Great Themes
of the Bible

Volume 1

W. Eugene March

Westminster John Knox Press
LOUISVILLE • LONDON

© 2007 W. Eugene March

Scripture quotations from the New Revised Standard Version of the Bible are copyright © 1989 by the Division of Christian Education of the National Council of the Churches of Christ in the U.S.A. and are used by permission.

Book design by Sharon Adamns
Cover design by Eric Walljasper, Minneapolis, MN
Cover art: Champaigne, Jean-Baptiste de (1631-1684). Sermon on the Mount. Oil on canvas. Reunion des Musées Nationaux/Art Resource, NY.

First edition
Published by Westminster John Knox Press
Louisville, Kentucky

This book is printed on acid-free paper that meets the American National Standards Institute Z39.48 standard. ∞

PRINTED IN THE UNITED STATES OF AMERICA

07 08 09 10 11 12 13 14 15 16 — 10 9 8 7 6 5 4 3 2

Library of Congress Cataloging-in-Publication Data

March, W. Eugene (Wallace Eugene)
    Great themes of the Bible / W. Eugene March. — 1st ed.
       p. cm.
    ISBN-13: 978-0-664-22918-4 (alk. paper)
    ISBN-10: 0-664-22918-2 (alk. paper)
  1. Bible—Theology. 2. Theology, Doctrinal. I. Title.

BS543.M37 2007
230'.041—dc22

                                                  2006048998

To Lynn
As we find new life together

Contents

Preface

The biblical story is rich. It was developed over the course of slightly more than a thousand years. The exact number of authors who contributed to the Bible is unknown. The precise historical setting of many of the writings is unknown. The meaning of a number of Hebrew, Aramaic, and Greek terms that appear in the original text is debated. And still the Bible is the most quoted, the most discussed, the most influential book in Western culture, and thus most worthy of careful consideration.

This first of three volumes dedicated to the exploration of some thirty-nine great themes that span the Old and New Testaments is aimed at enabling the educated, serious student of the Bible to gain insight into how various topics are presented in Scripture. There is no effort to "prove" or "defend" the authority of the Bible, though that is a worthy task. Rather, the importance of the material is assumed and approached accordingly.

The equal value of both testaments is likewise assumed. Sometimes the traditional terminology of Old Testament and New Testament is employed. At other points some newer terms are used, such as First Testament and Second Testament. Also, BCE (Before the Common Era) and CE (Common Era) are used in place of BC (Before Christ) and AD (Anno Domini) in keeping with the present scholarly consensus.

Matters of scholarly interpretation are not, for the most part, discussed in any great detail. They may inform the presentation, but they are not the focus of this study. One particular position is of some importance, however. At the time of Jesus and the development of the New Testament, neither Judaism as it is now known nor Christianity as a religion existed. These two great religious traditions developed in parallel beginning in the second century of the Common Era. Thus, when English translations speak of "Jews" they are being somewhat anachronistic. In the Bible "Christians" and "Jews" have far more in common than might be presumed on the basis of current history. The recognition of this important fact is crucial for understanding the social context and the writings that came out of that era, particularly when considering the Second Testament.

It is the hope of the author that this work will enable those interested in gaining a greater understanding of the Bible, which serves as the foundation of Christian discipleship. Thanks are due to the members of the March-Hester adult church school class of Highland Presbyterian Church in Louisville, Kentucky, for reviewing, discussing, and offering suggestions to the author concerning the content of most of this book. Also, to those of Westminster John Knox Press who provided invaluable technical assistance, and particularly to editor Donald K. McKim for his encouragement and understanding, thank you.

Chapter One

God

I n a book on themes of the Bible, it may seem strange to begin with God. God is hardly a "theme." God is the living source of grace and life that animates the world and offers comfort and guidance to millions of believers. God is better called "person" or "subject" than "theme." God cannot be objectified or defined or fully described in human language. God is richer than the stories told about God, greater than the experiences ascribed to God. God is God, and that is all there is to say!

Nonetheless, in a book dealing with the great themes of the Bible, it is important to trace the rich variety of witness offered concerning the living God in order to begin to comprehend the one whom the Bible says is the "main player" across the centuries of the divine/human drama that fills its pages. What's more, it is important to remember that the God of the Old (or First) Testament is the same as the God of the New (or Second) Testament, at least so far as the New Testament is concerned. The Bible does not support the widely held opinion that the God of the Old Testament is a God of wrath while the God of the New Testament is a God of grace. The God and Father of Jesus Christ is the God of Israel and Creator of the universe and all that is in it.

The Names of God

The General Name

The English word "god" is a general word for any divine being. While those who cherish the Bible may understand "god" to refer usually to the God of Israel and the Father of Jesus, the term itself is nonspecific. "Deity" could be its substitute in many instances. The Hebrew word for which "god" is the translation, *El* (with its plural *Elohim*), is also a general word for a divine being, though within some Semitic religious traditions, *El* is also a proper name of one of the chief deities. In Greek, the term for "god" is *theos* and, like *El*, usually is a general word for deity.

These terms were used in the ancient world within an assumed context of what we call polytheism. There was a whole company, a pantheon, of deities, gods and goddesses, who interacted with each other and on occasion with humankind. Each of these deities had a name and had to be addressed accordingly. The ancients did not assume that one word, *El* or *theos*, was sufficient to refer to the multiplicity of the gods, quite unlike the way we, in English, regularly use the term "God" to include the totality of the divine.

This language problem is important for at least two reasons. First, our translations of the Bible often disguise the vast difference between the theological perception that prevailed at the time of its writing and those that are common in predominantly Western culture. The reality of a multiplicity of divine beings was assumed and not debated. The Bible may warn against worshiping other deities, denying their power, but it generally leaves unchallenged the basic assumption of their existence. Second, as will be seen below, personal names are quite essential in talking about the work and character of the God of Israel. The God of Israel and Father of the Lord Jesus Christ was not simply a divine being with no distinct identity, but rather a personal deity with a very special personal name.

The Covenant Name

Clearly the most distinctive personal name by which the God of Israel was to be addressed was YHWH, the so-called sacred Tetragrammaton ("four-letter word"). The exact pronunciation has been lost because during the latter years of biblical tradition, out of respect for and the desire not to profane the name, the scribes ceased pronouncing it. When they read the Bible, they used terms like "Lord" or "the Name" when the text had "YHWH." Indeed, already by the third century BCE the earliest Greek translation of the Old Testament (the Septuagint) used the Greek word *kurios* (lord) each time the sacred name was encountered.

In English there have been two main efforts at suggesting the pronunciation of the Tetragrammaton. One suggestion has been "Jehovah," based on a use of vowels inserted quite late in the textual tradition (actually the vowels from the Hebrew word for "Lord") with the preserved consonants YHWH. The term "Jehovah" is not really possible by the rules of Hebrew pronunciation, but the tradition has continued nonetheless.

"Yahweh" has been the other major suggestion. Modern biblical scholars, noting Hebrew terms such as *hallelujah* (literally, "praise Yah") found in a number of psalms (e.g., 146:1; 147:1) and Hebrew names like Isaiah (literally, "Yah is salvation") and Elijah (literally, "my God is Yah"), have surmised that the first syllable of the divine name is "Yah." The second syllable is then assumed to be "weh" on the basis of verbal forms that might have been used. The case for the pronunciation is persuasive, but the meaning of the term created, "Yahweh," remains open for debate.

Some light is shed on the enigma of the covenant name when one examines the central biblical passage where the revealing of the sacred name is recounted. While tending the flock of his father-in-law Jethro in the region of Horeb, Moses encounters God (Exod. 3:1–12). Moses is instructed to go to Egypt to seek the release of God's enslaved people. Moses wants to know God's name in order to be able to identify God and to give Moses some authority when he speaks to the people to whom he has been sent. To Moses' inquiry the following exchange takes place:

> God said to Moses, "I AM WHO I AM." He said further, "Thus you shall say to the Israelites, 'I AM has sent me to you.'" God

also said to Moses, "Thus you shall say to the Israelites, 'The
LORD [YHWH], the God of your ancestors, the God of
Abraham, the God of Isaac, and the God of Jacob, has sent
me to you.'" (3:14–15)

The Hebrew word translated by the Greek Septuagint (and most
modern English versions) as "I AM" is a verbal variant from the
root of the word that constitutes the sacred name YHWH. There
continues to be debate as to the best translation. Many prefer
something like "I cause to happen what happens" or "I bring into
being whatever exists" or "I am present," rather than the static
sounding "I am" implied by the Greek. Whatever decision is
made, the important point is that this etymological issue is never
mentioned again in the Bible.

What YHWH did was what was definitive, not what the name
might theoretically mean. And what YHWH did was deliver
Israel from slavery in Egypt (Exod. 6:1–15:27). What YHWH did
was establish a covenant with Israel, giving instruction on how to
live in community (Exod. 19:1–24:18). What YHWH did was
promise the continuation of the gracious, forgiving, divine presence with the people as they traveled through the wilderness and
to the land of Canaan (Exod. 34:1–35). What YHWH did was
establish justice, care for the needy, work toward peace, and provide security and ample resources for the people (Pss. 146–147).
And when the Gospel of John presents Jesus saying "I am" repeatedly, the person and deeds of the covenant God YHWH are
intended to be remembered (John 4:26; 6:20, 35; 8:12, 58; 10:11;
11:25; 13:19; 14:6; 15:1; 18:5–6). Similarly, when the Second Testament writers refer to Jesus Christ as "Lord," the memory of
God's covenantal name is being recalled.

Names Appropriated from Canaanite Sources

As the tradition is remembered, prior to Moses especially, there
were a number of names of deities in the land that later came to
be claimed in reference to YHWH. Many used the general term
El as part of the name. *El Olam* ("Everlasting God") was associ-

ated with the sanctuary at Beersheba (Gen. 21:33). *El Bethel* ("God of Bethel") was remembered at Bethel (Gen. 35:7). At the spring Beer-lahai-roi, *El Roi* ("God who sees") was encountered (Gen. 16:13). *El Shaddai* ("God of the mountain" or possibly "God of the breasts"), usually rendered as "God Almighty" in English translations, probably referred to a deity associated with a particular mountain range (Gen. 49:24–25).

The plural form of *El*, *Elohim*, has a distinctive usage in the Old Testament. While in some instances the term simply refers to a multiplicity of (usually pagan) deities (e.g., Exod. 12:12; 18:11; Ps. 82:1), in most places the term is used in a singular sense as a reference to the one God to be identified as YHWH. Grammarians call this a "plural of majesty" and understand it to indicate something like "Most Divine God." When *Elohim* is so used, it refers to the totality of God, the fullness of the Divine. In the historical tradition of the First Testament, the term was most used prior to the revelation of the name of YHWH to Moses in Exodus (Gen. 1:26; 20:13; 35:7; cf. Exod. 3:15; 6:2–3).

While initially these names probably designated Semitic deities unrelated to YHWH, they were appropriated by the Israelites and, over the course of time, came to be understood as referring to the only God worthy of worship, namely, YHWH. Deities originally associated with natural phenomena and a particular place came to be interpreted as different manifestations of YHWH, who had a close, covenantal relationship with Israel's forebears (Abraham and Sarah, Isaac and Rebekah, Jacob, Leah, and Rachel), moved about with them (being unbound to any one particular place), and demonstrated divine power in providing protection and guidance to them.

One further term may have been drawn originally from the broader Northwest Mesopotamian setting, namely, "Rock." In Akkadian (ancient Assyrian and Babylonian) prayers, "great mountain" was a term sometimes used to refer to the deity. Also, in Israel's prayer traditions God is called "Rock" (e.g., Pss. 18:2, 31; 19:14; 28:1; 78:35). The prophet Isaiah used "Rock" as an epithet for God several times (Isa. 17:10; 26:4; 30:29). In one of the earliest traditions, Yahweh is praised as the Rock who gave birth to his people (Deut. 32:18). Further, Israel's Rock provided security and stability (Deut. 32:4, 15, 30–31). While the term may sound impersonal in English, the activities ascribed to the "Rock" are quite personal and are in accord with the other language for God already noted.

Metaphors for God

Besides the names used in reference to God, the Bible also uses numerous metaphors and epithets to describe the variety of ways that God interacts with humankind. Only a few of the more frequently used will be considered, but they will be instructive of the manner in which God was perceived and remembered.

From the social context of governance at least three terms emerged. First, there is the term "king." Across the ancient world "king" was a primary referent for a deity. Obviously the existence of earthly kings suggested that the gods were like kings, the guardians of the public welfare and enforcers of justice. Each nation or city-state had a divine king who was the special patron of that people. Israel was no different. The term "king" (or in its verbal form "to reign/rule") is often used in the book of Isaiah to extol Israel's God (Isa. 6:1, 5; 41:21; 43:15; 44:6) and declare Yahweh's reign over all the earth (Isa. 52:7, 10). Allusion to the reign of God is also found frequently in the Psalms (cf. Pss. 5:2; 29:10; 44:4; 68:24; 95:3; 97:1; 99:4; 146:10). Jesus announced the imminent coming of the reign (the kingdom) of God during the course of his public ministry (Matt. 6:10; 16:26; Mark 1:15; 9:1; Luke 9:27; 11:2), and the first generations of disciples continued the message (cf. Acts 8:12; 19:8; 1 Cor. 6:9; Gal. 5:21; Rom. 14:17; Rev. 11:15; 12:10; 22:5).

A second term closely related to "king" and widely used is "shepherd." In ancient Middle Eastern societies it was common to refer to the ruler as "shepherd." In the ancient law code of the Babylonian king Hammurabi (1792–1750 BCE), the king is designated "shepherd" of the people, their guardian and protector.

Likewise, Yahweh is called "Shepherd" (Gen. 49:24; Pss. 23:1; 80:1), and the people of Israel are "the sheep of his pasture" or his "flock" (Pss. 79:13; 95:7; 100:3). Modern readers may initially understand "shepherd" as a pastoral reference, but in the ancient world, when used in connection with God, the metaphor was intended to recall God's careful, reliable governance of the people. A third term drawn from this same social sphere is "judge." Before there were "kings" in Israel, there were leaders called "judges" who led the people in times of war and governed them. Their tasks included deciding issues of justice (Judg. 4–12). Thus, it was natural for God to be called "Judge" (Gen. 18:25; Isa. 2:4; 33:22; Ps. 94:2; Acts 10:42). This term was not as widely utilized as "king" or "shepherd," but it was a powerful symbol of God's protection and concern.

From the realm of family and kinship several important terms were drawn. One of the most important is "father." This term was used early in Canaanite religion in reference to El as the "father" of the gods and in Babylonian hymns to refer to the deity as the "Father of the Land." In later biblical texts God is called "Father" (Isa. 63:16; 64:8; Mal. 1:6). It is also interesting that the relationship between God and the Davidic dynasty is described in "father/son" language (2 Sam. 7:14–15; Ps. 2:7). This mirrors the manner in which some international political treaties of the time described the suzerain as "father" and the vassal as "son." While drawn from the family sphere, this use of "father/son" is clearly political in intent.

The term "mother" is not directly used of God, but feminine and maternal images are. One of the basic words signifying divine "mercy" also means "womb." God's "womblike," "motherly concern," God's mercy, is repeatedly mentioned (e.g., Exod. 34:6; Pss. 86:15; 111:4; Jonah 4:2). Further, in Isaiah God is compared to a nursing mother (Isa. 49:15), a woman in labor (Isa. 42:14), and a mother who comforts her child (Isa. 66:13).

In the New Testament, "Father" is used more frequently in reference to God and takes on a special significance because of Jesus' use of the term. While Jesus used the same language for God as

the Old Testament when quoting or referring to the earlier tradition (Matt. 11:25; 27:46; Mark 5:19; 13:20; 15:34; Luke 10:21;
22:69), he apparently preferred "Father," especially according to
the Gospel of John (e.g., John 5:17–24, 43–45; 6:27, 37, 44–46).
The Aramaic term for "father," *abba*, however, is found only three
times in the New Testament: once in the Synoptic Gospels (Mark
14:36) and twice in Paul's writings (Rom. 8:15; Gal. 4:6). Though
it has become commonplace for commentators to suggest that
abba was almost equivalent to "daddy" in the contemporary North
American context, that interpretation has been abandoned in
more recent scholarship. Actually, rather than being informal and
familiar, the term was one that expressed great respect and love
for God and emphasized the obedience and trust Jesus had as
"son." "Father" clearly underscores recognition of both the
authority and the personal nature of God.

Two epithets found in some of the later literature of the Old
Testament that have continuing relevance are "Creator" and
"Redeemer." Both are used extensively in Isaiah 40–55, often
ascribed to the "Babylonian Isaiah" or "Second Isaiah" (e.g., Isa.
40:28; 41:14; 43:1, 14–15). God's work as creator became especially important as a result of Israel's close encounter with Babylon, where the Babylonian god Marduk was praised as creator.
The work of the "Creator" by the power of the divine word is
described in Genesis (1:3, 6, 9, 11, 14, 20, 24, 26; cf. John 1:1–5).
As "Redeemer" God exercised a family responsibility. The head
of a family was expected to rescue or ransom other members of
the family who were taken into slavery. Isaiah proclaimed that in
the past God had rescued Israel from enemies and from perilous
situations and could be relied upon to do so again (e.g., Isa.
41:10–14; 43:1–7).

The Manifestations of God

The God revealed in the Bible is never fully disclosed. In the
midst of God's self-revelations only certain aspects of God are
shared with humankind. The single most important revelatory

event in the Old Testament was the release of Israel from Egypt. Under the inspiration of God, Moses led the people out of bondage. Israel learned a great deal about God's power and intention toward them when they escaped the chariots of Pharaoh at the waters of the Reed Sea ("Red Sea" in the Septuagint; see Exod. 14–15). The "exodus" has been remembered as part of the Passover festival to this day. God acted because God heard the cries of distress from the people (Exod. 3:7), but as important as that is, little more is revealed about God and nothing concerning the essence of God.

At the great theophany (the appearance of God) at Sinai, the people recognized the glory and holiness of God. They were afraid to approach the mountain and were in fact warned to stay at a distance (Exod. 19:12–18, 24). Moses was allowed to draw near to God, not to see God but only to hear God's voice (Exod. 19:20–25; 33:17–22). When the people left Sinai, they followed the "ark of the covenant" through the wilderness, with God's glory made visible in the fire and column of smoke that accompanied the ark (Num. 10:33–36). But they did not comprehend the full nature of God.

In the prophetic traditions of Israel, God was encountered primarily through the divine word that came to particular prophets. Amos recognized the great anger that God had for those who exploited the poor and ignored matters of justice (Amos 2:6–8; 5:21–24). Isaiah understood the judgment that God would level on Israel for its misdeeds (Isa. 5:1–7). Jeremiah became convinced that there was no hope of escaping disaster apart from an act of repentance that the people seemed incapable of rendering (Jer. 7:1–34). But Jeremiah also envisioned a day beyond the disaster when a new covenant of forgiveness would be fashioned by God (Jer. 31:31–34). Isaiah proclaimed a day of divine joy when renewal would be realized (Isa. 55:1–13). Even in Amos there is the announcement of a day of restoration (Amos 9:11–15).

But the prophets did not present a systematic statement about the essence or attributes of God. They said little or nothing about their own personal experiences of God. Rather they shared words about the things that mattered to God: anger and forgiveness, sorrow and rejoicing, abandonment and faithfulness, concealment and transparency, each an aspect of the way God was experienced, but never the wholeness of who God is.

In the New Testament the same God is praised and obeyed. But more, the Second Testament testifies that God's very Word was manifest in the flesh of Jesus of Nazareth (John 1:14–18). Jesus embodied the agenda of God for the care of the poor and the release of all the imprisoned (Luke 4:18–19). Jesus was love incarnate, but his closest disciples did not recognize who he was until after God raised him from the dead (Matt. 28:1–20; Luke 24:1–49; John 14:1–14; 20:1–29). The incarnation of God in Jesus could have been anticipated—after all, God most often interacted with Israel in the same ways another human might. But while God was incarnate in Jesus, much mystery remains, and with the apostle Paul we await that day when we will see face to face (1 Cor. 13:12).

Some Concluding Reflections

So who is the God of the Bible? God is clearly the "main character" the Bible intends to put forward. From the first encounter with humankind in the garden of Eden in Genesis to the final coming of the heavenly city of God at the conclusion of Revelation, God is at the center of the story. The Bible is about God and the way God is related to the human family and all the universes that came into being at God's word.

God is presented in the Bible in very personal terms. God has a personal name, YHWH. God is every bit as complicated as any individual we may know. As with another person, we never fully understand or comprehend God. YHWH sometimes seems distant, at other times close (perhaps even too close when we are in the wrong). YHWH displays joy, patience, anger, disappointment, acceptance, disapproval, just like other people we know. And sometimes, just when we think we have God figured out, God does the totally unpredictable and intervenes in our world and rearranges our politics or even raises someone from the dead.

YHWH is the God of Old Testament and New Testament people. Indeed, YHWH is Lord of all the people of the world.

God's many names and the numerous metaphors used to allude to YHWH inform us about the things that matter to God. We never see God fully. We never are invited in the Bible to somehow blend into the essence of God. But God is not a remote First Cause or the Unmoved Mover either. God is Father/Mother, King, Shepherd, Rock, and in Jesus Christ God is present in a unique and startling way.

Questions for Discussion

1. What is important about knowing that God has an actual, personal name in the Bible? How can we enrich our use of "God" in reference to the Divine?

2. How does the use of many different names and metaphors for God help us to recognize the many ways God encounters us? Which of these are most important to you? Why?

3. What do we actually know about God from the names, metaphors, and manner of encounters between God and humankind? What don't we know?

4. If someone asked you, "Who is the God of the Bible?" what might you say?

Chapter Two

Covenant

In the Bible, the language and metaphor of covenant provide one of the primary ways of describing God's relationship with humankind. A covenant is an agreement or contract akin to a marriage, a compact, an adoption decree, or a political treaty. The English term "covenant," derived from the Latin *convenire* via the Old French *convenir*, essentially means a "coming together," a "solemn agreement." A covenant identifies the parties in a relationship, outlines their respective responsibilities, and indicates the consequences of breaking the agreement. Covenants can be between two individuals or between two (or more) nations. Covenants can be relatively simple or highly complex.

In the Bible, the fact that God established covenants with human beings indicates clearly the divine desire for relationship. The use of covenant as the proper instrument by which God could relate to human beings was important. Covenants reflected the real social world in which the people lived. Their use as symbols testified to God's intention that humans would readily understand the relationship. God was always depicted as the gracious initiator of the covenants. It is instructive to consider the variety of covenantal forms used. From the beginning to the end, the Bible presents a series of covenants as a means of depicting the deep and ongoing commitment and love that God has for humankind.

The Covenant at Sinai

The covenant that God made with Israel through the mediation of Moses at Mount Sinai (Horeb) is the predominant covenant in the Bible. As the Old Testament is now organized, there are reports in the narrative of several covenants that precede that of the Sinai covenant, but in the tradition as a whole the Sinai covenant is considered most important and receives special attention (see Exod. 19–40; Deut. 5–28).

In the ancient Near East there were a number of different covenantal forms employed in various social contexts. Israel used the social customs and language of their time, and by analogy used them to describe their relationship with God. One such covenantal form was that of the suzerainty treaties used in the fourteenth and thirteenth centuries BCE by the Hittites, and by the Assyrians in the eight and seventh centuries BCE. These treaties or covenants followed a traditional format. The covenant God enters with Israel at Sinai appears similar to them in many respects.

The structure of the biblical treaty (covenant) is not exactly like that of the extrabiblical documents uncovered, but it does reflect three of the more typical elements. First, there is a statement of stipulations imposed by the more powerful king (the "suzerain," sometimes called "father") upon the less powerful king (the "vassal," sometimes called "son") with assurances of protection and support in exchange for loyalty and (usually) tribute. In the biblical covenant this takes the form of God's declaration of what we now know as the Ten Commandments (Exod. 20:2–17; Deut. 5:6–21). These are the essential "requirements" of the covenant. Second, there are witnesses (often the deities of the respective parties) summoned to acknowledge the formation of the treaty/covenant. In the biblical account, since there was no pantheon of deities upon which to call, this element is reduced to the repeated assertion that God alone is the guarantor of the covenant, with heaven and earth as witnesses (Exod. 34:10; Deut. 30:15–20). Third, most of the treaties have a long list of curses attached to remind the parties of the consequences of breaking the terms of the treaty. The biblical covenant continues this tradition (Deut. 27–28).

The covenant at Sinai, sometimes called the Mosaic covenant because of the central role played by Moses, is an obligatory covenant. That is to say, there are obligations attached to the covenant. God graciously offered the covenantal relationship, but expectations were placed upon the people. They were reminded of this when they "ratified" the agreement (Exod. 24:3–8; Deut. 26:16–19). In the course of time, the prophets used Israel's failure to meet these obligations as a basis for announcing divine judgment upon God's people.

The prophetic critique of God's people is seen most clearly in Isaiah and Jeremiah. They based their judgment directly on the people's failure to live in accordance with the Mosaic covenant. Isaiah chastised his people for their failure to maintain God's way: "Wash yourselves; make yourselves clean; remove the evil of your doings from before my eyes; cease to do evil, learn to do good; seek justice, rescue the oppressed, defend the orphan, plead for the widow" (Isa. 1:16–17; cf. Amos 5:14–15). The prophet likened Israel to a worthless vineyard that produced oppression rather than the justice and righteousness God expected of the people (Isa. 5:1–7). Echoing a complaint earlier voiced by the prophet Amos, Isaiah lamented the exploitation of the poor by the rich and the continued misrepresentation of evil as good (Isa. 5:8–10, 20; cf. Amos 2:6–8; 5:6–7; 8:4–6). Further, the political intrigues of the king and the leaders struck Isaiah as a rejection of God and God's promise to maintain them (Isa. 7:10–8:15; 30:1–5).

Jeremiah was no less direct. With a long announcement of judgment, Jeremiah chastised the rulers and the people for refusing to follow God's ways (Jer. 2:4–37; cf. 5:1–31). Israel's rebellion took the form of participation in Canaanite fertility religion, disregarding the care of the poor, and forming numerous "covenants" (political treaties) with other nations, thereby demonstrating a lack of trust in God. God's people practiced the external forms of religion but did not incorporate God's intentions into their hearts. "Will you steal, murder, commit adultery, swear falsely, make offerings to Baal, and go after other gods that you have not known, and then come and stand before me in this house [the temple], which is called by my name, and say, 'We are safe!'—only to go on doing all these abominations?" (Jer. 7:9–10). Violation of the stipulations of the covenant could not go unanswered.

It is important in reflecting on the Mosaic covenant to remember at least two things. First, the covenant, while it did contain stipulations and laws, was enacted in divine grace. God had already rescued Israel from Egypt (grace) before setting forth the covenant at Sinai (law). While the apostle Paul centuries later argued against the "law" in favor of "grace" and "faith," his dispute was with one particular way some people during his time had come to understand "law" (Gal. 3:19–29; 4:1–5:12). Second, and related directly to the preceding, the "law" was not viewed as a burden by most people, but as a gracious guide. In the form of numerous instructions, God's way for human community was defined. To experience the wholeness that God desired for the people, the "statutes and ordinances" were essential (see Exod. 20:22–23:33; Deut. 12:1–26:15). But following the commandments does not provide a legalistic means of assuring God's blessing. Rather, ordering life in light of the commandments provides the best possibility for a just and compassionate community, a community that God promised when the covenant was established. A relationship of blessing was the goal God had in mind from the very beginning, and covenant was intended to ensure that relationship (Exod. 6:5–8; Lev. 26:3–13).

The Covenant with David

There is a second biblical covenant almost as important as that made at Sinai, namely, God's covenant with David. The narrative describing the establishment of this covenant is found in 2 Samuel 7. The Israelites had installed a king to rule over them following the pattern of the surrounding countries. Saul was the first king

(see 1 Sam. 8–12), but for a variety of reasons Saul's reign as king
was unsuccessful. David, son of Jesse, was anointed to replace Saul
(1 Sam. 16:1–13). David actually became king only after Saul and
his sons Jonathan, Abinadab, and Malchishua were killed in bat-
tle (1 Sam. 31:1–7). When he did begin his reign, he quickly con-
solidated his position by, among other things, establishing
Jerusalem as his new capital and by bringing the ark of the
covenant to be kept there (2 Sam. 5–6). At this point in David's
story the covenant with God was announced.

Nathan the prophet, a close counselor of King David, brought
the divine word in response to a plan that the king had disclosed,
namely, the plan to build a "house" (temple) for God where the
ark could be placed (2 Sam. 7:1–3). Nathan, in a dream, was told
to tell the king that he was not to build a house for God (2 Sam.
7:4–11). Rather, and herein the basic covenant was established,
God promised to build a "house" (dynasty) for David. By this
covenant God assured David that God would be a "father" and
David would be his "son" (cf. Ps. 2:7). Moreover, David's line
would be "established forever." Should one of David's posterity
sin against God, that "son" would be chastised but not rejected.
David's "house" would stand in perpetuity (2 Sam. 7:12–17).

While the technical Hebrew term for "covenant" (*berith*) is not
used in this inaugural passage, it is found in other places where the
covenant is remembered (2 Sam. 23:5; Ps. 89:3; Jer. 33:20–21).
Further, a distinctive Hebrew covenantal term, "steadfast love"
(*hesed*), which can also be translated as "devoted loyalty" or
"loving-kindness," is used (2 Sam. 7:15; Ps. 89:49). God's *hesed*,
God's devoted loving-kindness, was the foundation that held the
covenant solidly in place.

The covenant with David shares some of the same characteristics of the covenant made at Sinai. Both covenants were initiated
by God, and both use some of the terminology (particularly the
father-son metaphor) of well-attested political treaties of the time.
But the covenant with David has a distinct difference. There are
no stipulations or conditions imposed on the king. God simply
promised to uphold David and maintain an ongoing relationship

no matter what happened. This is in the form of what is known as a royal promissory grant. Such grants, often of land, were frequently given to persons who had shown special loyalty to the king, but the recipient was not required to do anything in return. The legal status of these covenants rested solely on the royal promise or pledge that accompanied their granting. God's covenant with David was of this promissory type, and God's oath was the guarantee.

In the course of history, several important changes were made by those who received and passed along the tradition of the originally unconditional promise given David by God. The Davidic dynasty lasted for over four hundred years (1000–587 BCE), a very long time indeed. But in 587 BCE the Babylonians captured Jerusalem and took the Davidic king of Judah into exile. For all practical purposes, David's "house" had reached its end. Thus, when after that disaster the materials that constitute the present books of 1–2 Kings were written (ca. 500 BCE), a condition was added to the originally unconditional promise: "If your [David's] heirs take heed to their way, to walk before me in faithfulness with all their heart and with all their soul, there shall not fail you a successor on the throne" (1 Kgs. 2:4; cf. 2 Sam. 7:14–16; and Ps. 132:12 with Ps. 89:30–32). This qualification of the promise was highly significant. Likewise, when the Chronicler, writing a century later (ca. 400 BCE) reported the covenant with David, the original clause concerning God's intention to forgive the sin of David's sons was omitted (cf. 1 Chron. 17:10–14 with 1 Sam. 7:14–16) and a condition requiring that the Davidic king keep the commandments was included (1 Chron. 28:6–7; cf. 1 Kgs. 2:4). The amendment of the originally unconditional covenant with David made it possible to understand and interpret the historical disaster that had come upon Judah. The kings had not maintained the covenant, and the nation therefore received divine chastisement (2 Kgs. 23:1–27; 25:1–21; 2 Chron. 36:13–21).

In one sense, the dynasty promised to David that would last forever (2 Sam. 7:16) can be said to have come to an end in 587. There was one brief reprise with Zerubbabel, the last direct descendant of David. For a short period (520–515 BCE), Zerubbabel exercised authority as a governor of Judea, a Persian province that was fashioned from the former southern kingdom, Judah (see Hag. 1:1; 2:2, 20–23; Ezra 3:2, 8; 4:1–3). He was the last Davidic "king," so to speak. But in another way, the promise continued to have power. It was projected into the future. Hope arose for an eventual restoration of autonomy under the auspices of a future son of David yet to come, a new "anointed one" or "messiah."

The prophet Isaiah laid the foundation for this extension into the future of the promissory covenant with David. Isaiah envisioned a time yet to come when peace and justice (Isa. 9:4–7; 11:1–9) would be fully established by one who was a shoot from "the stump of Jesse" (Isa. 11:1; cf. Jer. 23:5–6; Ezek. 34:23; 37:24–25). Later, as the earthly restoration of the Davidic dynasty seemed less and less likely, that hope became part of the "end-time" expectations associated with the conviction that at the end of the age God would, through the auspices of the Messiah, inaugurate a messianic age in which the full intention of God's reign would be realized. When the New Testament community formed, Jesus of Nazareth was recognized and proclaimed as the "Christ," the "Anointed," the "Messiah," the long hoped for "son of David" (Matt. 1:1–17; Luke 3:23–38). Though God's reign has not yet been fully realized, God's promise to David continues to empower and assure believers.

The Covenants with Abraham and Noah

There are two more promissory covenants reported in the Bible: one with Abraham and his family and the other with Noah. Though it is second in the narrative, we will begin with the covenant between God and Abraham, Sarah, and their offspring. Rather out of the blue, God made a promise to Abraham that he would have a large family, receive land, and become a blessing to others (Gen. 12:1–3). In terms of literary form, this clearly resembles the covenant made with David and sounds very much like the

Near Eastern royal land grants bestowed in recognition of great loyalty. This divine promise is found repeatedly through the book of Genesis (13:15–17; 15:5, 7, 18–21; 17:2–8; 22:17–18; 24:60; 26:2–4; 28:3–4, 13–15). It defines the narrative flow and underscores the conviction that God was at work guiding the patriarchs and matriarchs toward the divine goal. There are no stipulations or commandments, only the promise of God. This covenant was God's pledge to bless Abraham and Sarah for the sake of the larger human family of which they were a part.

There was a sign of acceptance of the covenant, however: the act of circumcision. Every male born into the covenant community was to be circumcised (Gen. 17:10–14). While the instruction concerning circumcision is a commandment, failure to observe it did not abrogate the covenant. Those who would not follow the instruction were individually to be "cut off" from the community (17:14), but God's promise to Abraham, Sarah, and their heirs remained as an "everlasting covenant" no matter what (17:7). It was an unconditional promissory covenant.

The covenant with Noah is also promissory in form. The covenant was made after the great flood had come to an end (Gen. 7:1–8:19). Divine punishment had fallen on the peoples of the earth because of their great wickedness (6:1–7). But in grace, God determined to preserve at least a remnant of humankind from destruction and thereby directed Noah to build a boat in which he, his family, and representatives of every living kind might be safe during the deluge (6:8–22). Noah did as instructed and survived along with those with him.

After the flood, God pledged never again to curse the ground despite the wicked inclination of humankind. Never again would God punish the world by flood (8:21). God directed Noah and his family to repopulate the earth (9:1, 7; cf. 1:28). Instructions concerning the shedding of blood were given (9:3–6). Then God's pledge was restated in the form of a covenant (9:8–11). There was a sign given with this everlasting covenant, namely, the rainbow that God placed in the heavens to be seen by all humankind for as long as the seasons last (8:22; 9:13–17). There is nothing that humans must do to ensure this covenant. It is God-given and divinely maintained. Yes, humans are to live in accord with God's ways, but their failure to do so will not abrogate God's promise (8:21; 9:20–23).

The covenants with Abraham and Noah are noteworthy for at least two reasons. First, they were made with persons who represent the human family in general. Later in history, Jews, Christians, and Muslims came to claim Abraham and Sarah as common progenitors. But in the story as preserved, Abraham and Sarah are first of all Mesopotamians who represent the human family in general, just as Noah and his family even more clearly do. Second, these covenants set the whole divine-human drama in the context of divine grace reaching out to an undeserving and unsuspecting humanity. To be sure, Noah and Abraham are noted for their faithful trust (Gen. 7:1; 22:12; Heb. 11:7–12), but God instituted the covenants strictly as an act of grace. Neither Abraham nor Noah earned God's care and commitment.

A New Covenant

The prophet Jeremiah understood God's people to be liable for breaking the covenant with God by disregarding the commandments given therein (Jer. 2:27; 7:1–15). Accordingly, when the Babylonian armies ravaged Judah in 597 and 587 BCE, Jeremiah interpreted their actions as the execution of divine judgment (Jer. 28–29; 37–40). From Jeremiah's point of view, the Sinai covenant was at an end.

Still, Jeremiah did not see a total rejection of God's relationship with God's people. God could, and Jeremiah believed would, restore the covenant in a new form. Jeremiah envisioned God establishing a relationship that would be internal. Rather than writing the law on tablets of stone, God would inscribe the divine law on the human heart, the seat of the human will. People would obey God's commandments because they wanted to, not because they had to. And the forgiveness of God was announced as the very foundation of this renewed covenant (Jer. 31:31–34).

In the New Testament community, Jeremiah's words were connected with Jesus. Paul remembered the institution of the Lord's Supper as involving the words of Jeremiah, with Jesus explicitly describing the cup as the "new covenant in my blood" (1 Cor. 11:23–26; cf. 2 Cor. 3:5–6). The writers of the Synoptic Gospels also associated the term "covenant" with Jesus' last meal with his disciples (Matt. 26:27–29; Mark 14:24–25; Luke 22:17–20). An extensive use of Jeremiah's words is found in the book of Hebrews, where Jesus' self-sacrifice is interpreted as the basis for a "new covenant" (Heb. 8:8–12). Further, though not directly related to the Jeremiah passage, it is often noted that in his Sermon on the Mount, Jesus redirected God's covenantal laws to the *hearts* of his followers (Matt. 5:3–7:12).

Apart from the passages noted above, explicit covenantal language seems otherwise to be largely missing in the New Testament. But what is often forgotten is that the term "testament" itself is based on a Latin term meaning "covenant." Thus, the Old and New Testaments could also be called the First and Second Covenants. Each testament describes the covenantal relationship of God with human beings using images and language that people in ancient times readily understood.

Some Concluding Reflections

"Covenant" is not a word used widely in contemporary conversation. "Treaty" or "contract" comes near to expressing what a biblical covenant is, but not always. There are some biblical covenants that the term "promise" best describes, but promises do not mean too much for many people today. Thus, in interpreting the significance of biblical covenants, the background must be understood and connecting points sought.

The biblical covenants share the form and language of ancient treaties and grants, but the conceptual base is somewhat different. In the Bible, God always initiates the relationship. Humans sometimes are assigned responsibilities, but divine mercy and forgiveness always sustain the endeavor. Though legal in form, biblical covenants are not legalistic in spirit. The commandments are intended as guides for the developing of better community, not loopholes to catch the inattentive.

Biblical covenants defined the relationships that were established between God and human beings. These relationships were varied and had different goals. To understand one covenant is to understand one aspect of divine-human dealings, not the total possibility. These covenants have a "past tense" in that they were historical, guiding real people in real situations. But they also have a "present and future tense" in that they continue to instruct, challenge, and encourage God's people in a world quite different from the one in which they were first formulated. Their power rests in God, who is portrayed as willing and eager to engage and commit to lasting, enriching relationships with undeserving and often unfaithful human beings, thereby bridging the loneliness and separation that plagues so many today. Being in covenant with God is life giving!

Questions for Discussion

1. How does the social background of a term like "covenant" enrich the meaning the word has for today?
2. What are the similarities and differences between the Mosaic and Davidic covenants? How does Jesus represent both traditions?
3. How are God's covenants with Noah and Abraham important today?
4. How does being in covenant with God provide direction and confidence to you today?

Chapter Three

Humanity

The second most widely encountered theme in the Bible, second only to "God," is "humanity." Humans, like God, appear repeatedly, from the beginning to the end of the Bible. The Hebrew term *'adam* and the Greek term *anthropos* usually refer to "man" in the generic sense, and in earlier English versions of the Bible "man" or "mankind" were the usual translations of those terms. In more contemporary translations, "human" or "humankind" or "human beings" or sometimes "person" are the words generally employed. There are other terms that differentiate humanity with regard to gender, but the emphasis in this chapter is on humankind as a whole.

Humankind, according to the Bible, is of utmost importance to God. Thus, God blesses humans with great abilities and opportunities. But God also has great expectations and, unfortunately as the Bible records, experiences great disappointments. Created in the "image of God" (Gen. 1:26) and only a "little less than the angels" (Ps. 8:5 KJV; cf. NRSV: "a little lower than God"), humans clearly have great potential before God and great responsibilities. In examining the commission given to humanity, both the capability and the performance of the human family warrant consideration. God has been described as eagerly desiring and pursuing relationship with humanity. But who are the humans that God seeks so persistently? What does the Bible tell us about humankind?

Created in the Image of God

There are two creation stories in Genesis (1:1–2:4a; 2:4b–25). The first is a majestic, carefully crafted declaration of the creative power of God's word. God speaks and the universe, the world, and all that lives in it takes on the ordered form we call "the creation" (Gen. 1:3, 6, 9, 11, 14, 20, 24, 26). The end of God's creative work is a day of rest, the seventh day, that, while not expressly stated, points toward the establishment of the Sabbath as a day to put labor aside and reflect on the goodness of God (2:2–3; cf. Exod. 20:8–11; Deut. 5:12–15).

On the sixth day, humankind is created by God's word (1:26–27). This is clearly the climax of the litany of God's creative acts. Humanity has a special place in the divine ordering of reality. Humans are given a special responsibility, namely, to "be fruitful and multiply, and fill the earth and subdue it; and have dominion over the fish of the sea and over the birds of the air and over every living thing that moves upon the earth" (1:28). The operative words are "fill" and "subdue"—important tasks!

The responsibilities assigned to humankind are completely in keeping with their uniqueness before God. According to Genesis, of all the creatures, humans alone are created in the "image" (Hebrew, *tselem*; Greek, *eikon*) and according to the "likeness" (Hebrew, *demut*; Greek, *homoioma*) of God (1:26). The first Hebrew term is most helpful in illuminating the author's metaphorical language. A *tselem* was an actual material statue or other physical representation of a deity or monarch that was placed in a temple or at a border to indicate the ownership of the particular sanctuary or land involved. "Images" of Marduk, the chief deity of Babylon, for instance, stood in important public places around the city and the empire. In later nonbiblical theological writings, the term *demut* has often been interpreted as referring to the inner character of humans, to the mind or the spirit for instance, but in Genesis the emphasis is more likely on the external and visible character of the term in keeping with the function of an "image."

Because humans are created in the image of God (Latin, *imago Dei*) they represent God wherever they are. They are like little statues of God reminding themselves and others of their Lord. But they are not static. Related as they are to God, they are also related dynamically to one another. They have been authorized to act on behalf of God as they "fill the earth and subdue it." They are given sexuality so that they may fill the earth. Their dominion is an extension of the divine, and that makes them all the more responsible before God (Gen. 9:3).

Being in the image of God means that humans have a special affinity with God. The biblical God, who is described as having love, compassion, faithfulness, and even anger (Exod. 34:6–7) is not surprising to those in God's image. That God could approach Abraham and Sarah in "human form" and enter into dialogue with them is plausible (Gen. 18:1–35). Further, it is quite understandable when the New Testament proclaims that Jesus is the visible "image of the invisible God" (Col. 1:15), transforming all who gaze upon him by God's power (Col. 3:1–17).

The issue is not whether humans can lose or destroy the image of God. They cannot, for they are forever creatures who are only a "little lower than God" and "crowned . . . with glory and honor" (Ps. 8:5). Rather, the issue is how well humans will represent God and carry out the dominion entrusted to them. Will they care for the creation or exploit it? Will they relate to one another with love or with disdain? In their successes and in their failures, they stand as reminders that this world belongs to God and is accountable to the Creator. Being in the image of God is wonderfully awesome and a little terrifying.

Earth Creatures

The second account of the creation of humanity begins at a totally different place. The scene opens with God addressing a pressing problem, a need for someone to till the ground (Gen. 2:5). To remedy this difficulty, the Lord God forms "man" (Hebrew, *'adam*), from the ground, from dirt or dust (Hebrew, *'adamah*), and breathes into *'adam* the breath of life (2:7). There is a deliberate wordplay with this use of *'adam* and *'adamah*. At the outset of the story, *'adam* is simply a creature fashioned from the ground, an "earth creature." As a potter shapes an earthen vessel, so God shapes *'adam*.

The unnamed earth creature was placed in a flourishing garden previously planted by God. The term *'adam* was not initially the proper name Adam that it later came to be (Gen. 4:25). The garden God provided had every type of tree good for food, but it also contained the "tree of life" and the "tree of the knowledge of good and evil" (2:8–9). The earth creature was given authority over the garden and had free access to all of it except for one tree, namely, the tree of the knowledge of good and evil (2:15–17). Of that tree, *'adam* was forbidden to eat.

The earth creature was initially alone. God recognized that this was not good and decided to provide a companion for *'adam*. God created one animal after another and allowed the earth creature to name each (2:18–20). But a suitable helpmate was not found. Then God put the earth creature, formed from the dirt of the ground, to sleep. God then extracted a rib and created an appropriate companion, an *'ishshah* (Hebrew for "woman" or "wife") for the *'ish* (Hebrew for "man" or "husband"). For the first time in the story the earth creature is differentiated into male and female. The man was pleased with the woman, and the two were at peace with one another and with God (2:18–25).

From this account of the origin of humanity, several observations are in order. First, humankind is totally dependant upon God for its origin. God willingly chose to create human beings and gave them community and provisions for a good life. Humankind is God's first and most important creation. But the claim here is theological, not scientific. In antiquity there were no arguments about whether or how the gods were responsible for creating the world, only debate about whose god was in fact the

Creator. Second, despite being fashioned by the hand of God, humankind has clear limitations. Humans were fashioned from the dirt of the ground. They are part and parcel of the rest of the created universe, and are a finite, to a certain degree fragile, part of the natural order. They cannot escape this and should not forget it. Third, they are creatures given the task of tilling the earth and caring for it. In that sense, this picture of the place of humankind in God's world is similar to that found in the first creation story. Caring for the garden requires the same level of responsibility and sensitivity as filling and subduing God's creation. Humanity has a task to perform on behalf of God. But the second account gives humanity a less majestic, more earthy character. Humans are made of the very ground they are responsible to till.

Human Wholeness

In the Bible, human beings are considered primarily in their body-spirit wholeness. That is to say, for the biblical writers there was not a bifurcation of "soul" from "flesh" commonly presumed today by large numbers of people in the West. A human being was a body animated by God's "breath of life," and therein a "living being" or a "living soul" (Gen. 2:7). The Hebrew term *nephesh*, sometimes translated as "soul," was understood as the life principle, but it could not be separated from the whole living creature. What had been dirt became an animated being, a living *nephesh*, when activated by God's breath. But unlike the term "soul" as used in much contemporary Western reflection, the *nephesh* was neither immortal nor separable from the body. A human being did not "have" a *nephesh*. A human being "was" a *nephesh*. Death meant that the animated body-soul combination called "human being" (*nephesh*) ceased to exist.

Living humans had the capacity to think, to feel, to plan, to act, but they did so in their wholeness. The terms rendered in English translation as "mind," "heart," "will," and "spirit" are practically interchangeable in Hebrew. And there is no Hebrew word that literally refers to "soul" as that English word is most commonly used. Humans were living beings by the power of God's breath alone. When that breath was removed, the human died—the whole human, not merely the flesh. This is the understanding of humankind reflected in the Old Testament.

Somewhere during the second century BCE, under the influence of Greek culture, a profound change in perspective was introduced. In the apocryphal book the Wisdom of Solomon, the Greek understanding of "soul" is first found in a Jewish writing. Though written for a Jewish audience, a dualism of a "perishable body" and an "immortal soul" is assumed, quite in opposition to long-standing tradition (Wis. 3:1–3; 9:15). By the time the New Testament appeared, the bifurcation of body and soul was taken for granted.

Nonetheless, because of the deep connection that the earliest Christian writers had with the Old Testament, tension existed. Sometimes the Greek term for "soul" (*psuche*, from which the English "psyche" is derived) is understood as a reference to the whole person (Acts 2:41). Sometimes it seems to mean more generally "life" (Mark 3:4). In Luke there are instances when it seems that people can preserve their "lives," their "souls," or "themselves," even beyond death (Luke 9:25; 12:4; 21:19). The adoption of the Greek notion of an immortal, imperishable soul in opposition to a finite, perishable body may not be totally accomplished in the New Testament, but when the apostle Paul tries to communicate the significance of the resurrection, he comes very close (1 Cor. 15:35–57). Of course, the very fact that he had to defend the Hebrew belief in the necessity of "resurrection" is testimony to the tension between Greek culture (the "soul" at death leaves the body, and that is good) and the Hebrew understanding that resurrection is necessary if one is to survive beyond death because the whole person dies (there can be no "person" or "soul" that has no body).

One other term should be considered in this discussion, namely, "spirit." After God shaped the earth creature, God animated '*adam* with divine "breath" (Hebrew, *neshamah*; Gen. 2:7) or "spirit" (Hebrew, *ruah*; 6:17). That spirit not only animates the human in whom it resides but it also enlivens all living things (6:17; 7:15). When the "spirit" is withdrawn, death comes (6:3). A person's "spirit" sometimes was understood as a source of emotion or desire or moral judgment, quite similar to the "heart" or "soul" (Isa. 26:9; 54:6; Ps. 32:2; 51:10). In the New Testament the Greek word *pneuma* is used regularly to translate the Hebrew *ruah*. As the church became more Gentile and less Jewish in its membership, in keeping with Greek culture, *pneuma* frequently referred to the "inner life" or "soul" of a person (1 Cor. 5:5; Gal. 6:18; Jas. 2:26) and carried with it a greater sense of permanence or immortality. With this change in perception the notion of the wholeness of a human being was challenged. Greek dualism pitted "flesh" against "spirit." While the Bible as a whole, including the New Testament, resists such a dualism, there is clearly tension in the later writings of the canon.

Humanity's Vulnerability

The Bible makes clear that the human condition is dangerously vulnerable. This is not simply the by-product of finiteness, though the unpredictable character of life certainly is a factor. Humans in one sense are quite frail (Ps. 103:13–16). But the vulnerability is much more profound. It is an inner matter that has to do with basic predisposition.

The Bible introduces the matter in the very beginning of the human story. Adam and Eve inhabited a beautiful garden with ample food for their needs. They could eat of anything in the garden except for the fruit of one tree, the tree of the knowledge of good and evil (Gen. 2:16–17). They disregarded God's directions, however, and succumbed to the temptation to eat the forbidden fruit (3:1–14). They acted freely but against the expressed will of God. By their act they became like God in knowing good and evil. As a result God decided to expel them from the garden before they could eat of the tree of life and become immortal (3:22–24). That did not solve the problem, though. Later, according to the story, God considered humanity and realized that "every inclination of the thoughts of their hearts was only evil continually" (6:5). God decided, therefore, to destroy humankind with a great flood (6:6–7). But the twisted inclination of humankind continued even after the flood, and God decided to acknowledge it and move on (8:21). The Bible never explains this inclination. Jeremiah the prophet recognized it when he said, "The heart is devious above all else; it is perverse—who can understand it?"(Jer. 17:9). Because of this inclination, humanity is in a vulnerable situation, with the possibility of self-destruction always close at hand.

The consequences of this vulnerability are cataloged through the pages of the Old and New Testaments. Immediately after Adam and Eve left the garden of Eden, Cain murdered his brother Abel (Gen. 4:8). Hosea the prophet observed of the situation in his time (the eighth century BCE) that "there is no faithfulness or loyalty, and no knowledge of God in the land. Swearing, lying, and murder, and stealing and adultery break out; bloodshed follows bloodshed" (Hos. 4:1b-2). A quarter-century later Isaiah the prophet castigated Jerusalem saying, "Your princes are rebels and companions of thieves. Everyone loves a bribe and runs after gifts. They do not defend the orphan, and the widow's cause does not come before them" (Isa.1:23).

The Second Testament continues the critique. Mark quotes Jesus, "For it is from within, from the human heart, that evil intentions come: fornication, theft, murder, adultery, avarice, wickedness, deceit, licentiousness, envy, slander, pride, folly. All these evil things come from within, and they defile a person" (Mark 7:21–23). And Paul warns the Galatians, "Now the works of the flesh are obvious: fornication, impurity, licentiousness, idolatry, sorcery, enmities, strife, jealousy, anger, quarrels, dissensions, factions, envy, drunkenness, carousing, and things like these" (Gal. 5:19–21). Such actions destroy individuals. Such actions destroy communities. Humanity is indeed vulnerable to destruction. Humankind stands under the judgment of God, for none is righteous in God's eyes (1 Kgs. 8:46; Job 4:17; 9:2; Rom. 3:20).

Humanity's Potential

Despite the predisposition in humans toward evil, they nonetheless have enormous potential for good. In sharp contrast to the works of the flesh, Paul can describe the fruit of God's Spirit to the Galatians as "love, joy, peace, patience, kindness, generosity, faithfulness, gentleness, and self-control" (Gal. 5:22–23). And he exhorts the Philippians: "Finally, beloved, whatever is true, whatever is honorable, whatever is just, whatever is pure, whatever is pleasing, whatever is commendable, if there is any excellence and if there is anything worthy of praise, think about these things" (Phil. 4:8). As clearly as Paul saw human weakness and the propensity to sin, he also recognized human potential for good. With the assistance of God, humankind could produce marvelous fruit.

From the beginning, the creature made in God's image had a special possibility. Humankind was given authority over creation (Pss. 8; 144:3). This fact demonstrates God's view of human potential. That humankind has not lived up to God's expectations does not alter the vision of their creation. When humans walk humbly before God and act justly and with kindness, God is pleased and things can go well (Mic. 6:8). People can, and some people do, live in accordance with the Ten Commandments (Exod. 20:2–17; Deut. 5:6–21). People can, and some people do, live with dignity and charity, and deal with others fairly and justly (Job 29:1–25; Prov. 31:10–31). People can, and some people do, make the Golden Rule their daily guide (Matt. 7:12; Luke 6:31).

In the New Testament, the final culmination of God's work with humanity is symbolized in the figure of the "last Adam" (1 Cor. 15:45). Jesus' work of obedience (Heb. 5:8–9; 10:5–9) brings the assurance of deliverance and restoration. Just as humankind bore the "image of the man of dust, we will also bear the image of the man of heaven," namely, Jesus Christ (1 Cor. 15:49). The lasting significance of humanity being created in the divine image is once again attested in Christ's identification as the "second man," the "second Adam." God's incarnation and saving acts came into visible presence in the person of a human being, thereby declaring the continuing value and potential of humanity.

Some Concluding Reflections

Humankind in the Bible is represented as the culminating achievement of God's creative action. Humans are the very image of God standing in the midst of the world reminding all that this world is God's territory. Unlike in some of the other creation stories found among the traditions of the peoples of the ancient Near East, humans are not viewed as the slaves of the gods but as the intended companions and confidants of the Creator of the universe. Humans were assigned the responsibility to care for the earth, exercising diligent and just dominion over all creation. They were to be God's agents, honored by their Creator and dignified by the assignment that was theirs.

God, according to the Bible, began the quest for relationship with humankind in the garden of Eden and will not be satisfied until the peace and harmony of that first garden are restored at the end of time in the new earth and the new Jerusalem (Rev. 21:1–27). God has never ceased to care for humankind, though divine punishment has sometimes fallen, but the relationship sought initially by God has yet to be fully realized.

Humanity was created in the image of God but at the same time was a creature of the earth. God's creative hand fashioned humankind as a potter might shape a vessel from the dirt of the ground. Then God breathed into this earth creature and it became a living being (Gen. 2:7). Humanity continues to depend upon God for its life's breath. Human life is relatively short when compared with the life span of a redwood or the seemingly endless endurance of a mountain. Human beings are of the earth and will return to the earth, and need continually to be reminded of that fact. Human beings are creatures fashioned by God—nothing more but also nothing less.

The tragic character, the vulnerability, of human life rests in the God-given capability to make free decisions and to act independently of God. In the story of the garden of Eden, God's creatures chose to act against God's explicit instructions. The immediate consequence was the acquisition by humankind of the capacity to discern good and evil. Therein began a struggle that continues, wherein humanity regularly makes the wrong choices, indeed, an inclination to do the wrong thing (Gen. 6:5; 8:21). Why this is true, and whether or how it is connected with the ability to know good and evil, is never fully clarified in the Bible and remains a topic of energetic debate. What is very clear is that humans more often than not fail to live in the manner that their Creator expected and continues to desire.

Questions for Discussion

1. What are the important points made by each of the two accounts of the creation of humankind as reported in Genesis 1–2? How do these accounts complement one another? How do they set the stage for the remainder of the biblical story?
2. How do you resolve the tension between the biblical assumption about the resurrection of the body and Greek assumptions about the immortality of the soul?
3. Is God responsible for the inclination toward evil of the human heart? Why or why not? Is free will related to this issue?
4. What are some of the good things that humans are capable of doing? Is every human act sinful? How does God enable humanity to move toward wholeness?

Chapter Four

Sin

"Sin" is a word that many modern people misunderstand, avoid, or ignore altogether. Even within some communities of faith, the fact of sin is often debated and frequently denied. But within the Bible, sin is both a necessary concept and a substantive reality. It is a necessary concept in the sense that much of the message of the Bible cannot be understood without the conviction that sin is a reality. It is a substantive concept in that it defines the human condition as significantly marred in its relationship with God. Sin is a primary theological issue.

Sin in the Bible refers both to a condition and to specific activities. The origin of sin is not explicitly stated, but the Bible recognizes it as part of the divine-human story from the very beginning and assumes it as being the universal experience of all humankind. Thus, it is important to understand what the Bible does say about sin, what it is and what we are to do about it, and especially how God views sin. The experience and consequence of sin provides the continuing context from which the biblical story unfolds.

Biblical Terminology for Sin

In the New Testament one basic term is used in reference to sin. This term, *hamartia*, at root means to "miss the mark," and it is used with reference to a number of different actions more carefully distinguished in the Old Testament. This one term, by and large, covers everything from ritual infractions to severe moral misbehavior. The apostle Paul offers perhaps the best insight into the essence of sin when he relates all sinful activity to some form of idolatry (Rom. 1:18–25). The most fundamental form of missing the mark is to substitute the worship of creature or created things for reverence for and obedience to the Creator of the universe. From this basic sin, according to Paul, all other particular sinful behavior flows.

The First Testament delineates sin into more specific categories. This can enable the sinner to recognize the numerous ways, the nuances, of disobedience, hopefully to avoid them. There are a large number of terms that relate to sin, perhaps as many as fifty. Here, however, five of the most frequent and important will be considered. The English translations of these terms often do not preserve the distinctions intended by the Hebrew. The same English words, "sin" or "fault" or "offense," may be used to translate quite different Hebrew terms, each of which has its own connotation.

The most general term in the Hebrew vocabulary for sin is *hata'*, which basically means to "go astray," "fail," or "err." At one level *hata'* can refer to things done quite unintentionally (Lev. 4:2). At the other extreme, however, Moses calls Israel's reprehensible worship of the golden calf *hata'* (Exod. 23:30). It is understandable, therefore, how the New Testament writers could use various forms of *hamartia* in much the same way to refer to all forms of sin.

A second term is *'awon*, often translated as "iniquity." The term can refer to specific wrongdoings. The prophet Jeremiah reprimands his people because "they all deceive their neighbors, and no one speaks the truth; they have taught their tongues to speak lies; they commit iniquity [*'awon*] and are too weary to repent" (Jer. 9:5). But it can also indicate the guilt that one incurs as a result of such misbehavior. One can be said to "bear iniquity," to stand "guilty" because of one's deeds (Num. 5:31). Finally, *'awon* is sometimes translated "punishment," for it can indicate the judgment that accompanies the misdeed (Ezek. 14:10). No single

English term can cover all the meanings that are encountered in the biblical text.

Another Hebrew term, *'asham*, in addition to *'awon*, is used almost exclusively with the meaning of "guilt." In Leviticus the term can refer to guilt incurred by unintentional sin (Lev. 4:13) and to the sacrificial act of purification intended to remove the guilt (4:14). In Numbers 5:6, if a person "wrongs another, breaking faith with the LORD, that person incurs guilt [*'asham*]." The term does not reflect a psychological state so much as a legal or relational condition.

A fourth, very strong term describing sin is *pasha'*, often translated "transgression." This word is drawn from the realm of international relations. When a vassal nation rebelled against its sovereign, that was *pasha'*. In response to Israel's continuous involvement in the worship of Canaanite fertility deities, Jeremiah says on behalf of God: "Why do you complain against me? You have all rebelled [*pasha'*] against me" (Jer. 2:29). To transgress, or to rebel, or to defy God was the most serious form of sinful action in the eyes of the Old Testament writers.

There is one other term that should be noted, *rasha'*, usually translated "wicked." This term characterizes both the actor as well as the sinful act. To sin is to act wickedly (2 Chron. 20:35). Impenitent sinners are considered wicked (Gen. 18:23). As a noun, this term is used frequently in Psalms and Proverbs to designate people, the wicked, who are in some way at enmity with God (e.g., Pss. 7:9; 9:16; Prov. 2:22; 4:14). This most common designation for sin signifies the seriousness with which sin was viewed. Wickedness alienated the sinner from God and was highly detrimental to the community. Deliberate rebellion against or disregard for God's way was reprehensible and was not to be dismissed lightly as just a mistake.

Sin's Origin

The Bible does not reveal the origin of sin. Throughout its pages, accounts about sinners and the negative results of sinning are regularly recorded. Sin is part of the context in which human life is conducted, but how this came to be is not explained.

There are two primary passages that interpreters have mined across the centuries in the quest of an adequate understanding of the origin of sin, with its ongoing capacity to disrupt and destroy individual lives and communities. The first is Genesis 6:1–8. This is an account of how the "sons of God," divine beings that inhabited God's heavenly court, took human women as wives (6:2). This commingling of the divine spirit with mortal flesh was offensive to God, who immediately limited the possible duration of life of any offspring to one hundred twenty years (6:3–4). As a result of these unauthorized unions "the LORD saw that the wickedness of humankind was great in the earth, and that every inclination of the thoughts of their hearts was only evil continually" (6:5). Even after the flood that was sent to eradicate this wickedness, however, the "inclination [Hebrew, *yetzer*] of the human heart" continued to be evil (6:6–7; 8:21).

During the intertestamental period (ca. 200 BCE–100 CE), there was much speculation about Genesis 6. One important book, *1 Enoch*, cited in the New Testament book of Jude as though it were Scripture (Jude 6, 14–15), gave an elaborate explication of the events of Genesis 6 as the source of sin in the world (1 En. 6–16).

Later Jewish interpreters concentrated on "the inclination [*yetzer*]" of the heart as the point of origin of sinful decision. They speculated on the existence of two inclinations in each individual, one that led to good and one that inclined toward evil. The good *yetzer* impels individuals into meaningful, constructive activities, while the evil *yetzer* seeks to distort the good into the bad, to mislead the individual into destructive behavior. In each person there is an ongoing struggle between these two inclinations, with the evil *yetzer* prevailing much of the time. The apostle Paul seems to have interpreted some of his own experience along these lines (Rom. 7:18–20). But while this exploration of the dynamics of individual sinful decision making was very helpful in understanding the tensions within the heart, and while it did absolve God from being responsible for sin, it did not actually solve the puzzle, for it did not disclose why the *yetzer* tended toward evil (Gen. 6:5; 8:21).

Within Christian circles, however, another line of interpretation developed concerning the origin of sin. Taking a different explication offered by Paul, namely, that Jesus Christ was the new Adam (Rom. 5:12–21), interpreters turned to Genesis 2–3. Nowhere in this passage is the actual language of sin employed. Nonetheless, the dynamics of sin are dramatically presented. Moving from temptation to disobedience to consequence, the destructive character of sinful action is portrayed.

At the conclusion of Genesis 2, "man" (Hebrew, *'ish*) and "woman" (Hebrew, *'ishshah*) are situated in God's garden (2:18–24). The man comes to be called "Adam" (2:20), and he names the woman "Eve" (3:20). They began their story in harmony with one another and with God, a reality attested with the simple observation that they "were both naked, and were not ashamed" (2:25). Within the garden they had access to all that they needed, and in abundance.

But there was one prohibition, and therein lies a possibility for disaster. One tree in the garden is placed off limits, namely, the "tree of the knowledge of good and evil" (2:17). Humans had the capacity to decide between right and wrong, but "the knowledge of good and evil" was the special knowledge of God alone. The existence of that beautiful tree with its wonderful fruit (3:6) proved too great a temptation. Egged on by a talking snake (that some later interpreters identified as a manifestation of the devil), Eve and Adam succumbed to temptation and disobeyed God's instruction (3:4–7). In so doing, according to Christian interpretation, the first act of sin was committed, though it was not named as such in the text. (Jewish commentators recognize a disruption in the human-God relationship, but they do not look to this passage for the origin of sin.)

It is important to consider what happened carefully. God had instituted a close personal relationship, based on mutual trust, with the representatives of humankind. But when God's goodness was questioned and the fruit of the one forbidden tree was tasted, the relationship of trust was severed. The sin was consummated in the act of eating, but it began in the loss of trust that God had, in fact, provided all that was good for his human creatures. At its most basic, then, sin is the result of human failure to live faithfully within the limitations set by God, with human beings believing somehow that there is something better that they, by their own power and wits, can attain.

The consequence of this first breach of trust was the loss of close relationship with God and eventually with others in the human family. The humans could not hurt God, in one sense, but they did alienate God. The innocence in which they first lived was gone. Hubris, or pride, became a daily companion. God recognized what Adam and Eve had done and laid punishment on the serpent, Eve, and Adam (3:13–19). Further, God expelled the humans from the protection and abundance of God's garden (3:23–24). From that point on, the biblical story recounts a tale of sibling rivalry and murder (4:8–16), clan warfare (Gen. 4:23–24), and eventually the wickedness that brought the great flood (6:5–7).

This account does not explain why or how sin came to be such a universal experience. It does place the fault, however, clearly with humankind. There has been much speculation about whether this is rightly called "the fall" and whether the propensity for sin is somehow passed along from generation to generation biologically or by social mechanism. Among those who believe the Bible, however, there is no debate about the fact that sin is real and that sin has had terrible consequences for human individual lives and for community.

Specific Sinful Activities

The Bible offers numerous examples of behavior deemed to be wicked. In the First Testament there are two general types of behavior that are noted. First, there is a great deal of attention focused on a number of ritual regulations. Prescription for the proper preparation of and offering of sacrifices is made (Lev. 1–4). Stipulations concerning clean and unclean foods are set forth

(Lev. 11). Rules concerning a variety of necessary purification procedures are carefully elaborated (Lev. 12–15). Violation of any of these numerous regulations was considered sin.

What is important to note about the type of sin related to ritual laws is that motivation was significant. Distinction was made between doing something intentionally or unintentionally. Accidental violation of these rules, whether by ignorance or inattention, was dealt with quite differently from intentional disregard for God's way. For unintentional sins there were various offerings that could be made to restore the proper relationship with God (Lev. 4, 16). At the same time, these sacrifices returned the sinner to his or her proper place in the community. While many have long since come to consider these ritual violations no longer applicable in contemporary society, they nonetheless remind readers of the Bible that all aspects of life are important to God and that willful disregard of God's way will lead to alienation both from God and from one's community.

A different type of sinful behavior is that which results from willfully disobeying what are now considered the Bible's moral admonitions. The Ten Commandments (Exod. 20:2–17; Deut. 5:6–21; cf. Lev. 19:11–18; Jer. 7:9; Ezek. 18:5–18; 22:6–22; Hos. 4:2; Pss. 50:16–19; 81:9–10; Mark 10:19; Luke 18:20; Rom. 13:9) are the most obvious and well-known regulations of this sort that come to mind. One does not accidentally murder, commit adultery, steal, or defame another. These sinful acts are intentional, and they destroy individuals and communities.

While few would defend the activities prohibited in the Ten Commandments, some would prefer to call them antisocial acts rather than use the biblical term "sin." But from the Bible's point of view, every failure to follow God's way is a sin. And these particular acts, particularly if there is no repentance, reflect an attitude on the part of the sinner that is itself a grave sin. They declare that the sinner believes himself or herself outside God's reign. The sinner is wiser, more powerful, more astute than God, and can do as she or he pleases. This is in essence a form of idolatry and is perhaps the ultimate sin (cf. the "unpardonable sin" warned against in Mark 3:28–30). Those who adopt this attitude and mode of action, the Bible says, are "fools" who say in their hearts, "There is no God" (Pss. 14:1; 53:1; cf. Prov. 1:7; 2 Sam. 13:11–14; Jer. 29:23; Rom. 1:21–23).

The apostle Paul categorizes all sin, finally, as the result of idolatry. Because humans "did not see fit to acknowledge God" they do "every kind of wickedness, evil, covetousness, malice. Full of envy, murder, strife, deceit, craftiness, they are gossips, slanderers, God-haters, insolent, haughty, boastful, inventors of evil, rebellious toward parents, foolish, faithless, heartless, ruthless" (Rom. 1:28–31; cf. 1 Cor. 6:9–10; Gal. 5:19–21; Col. 3:5, 8; 1 Tim. 1:9–10; 6:4–5; 2 Tim. 3:2–4; Titus 3:3). These are deliberate acts that demonstrate the lack of human trust in God and obedience to God's way. In the divine economy of judgment, humans are punished by the outcome of the sinful things that they do. Sometimes this is experienced as the absence of God in their midst. At other times it is the terrifying sense of God's holy presence with which people must deal.

But if Paul saw sin as the inevitable result of idolatry, he also spoke of sin as a power that enslaved humankind, a power that only God could defeat (Rom. 6:12–14). In one sense the urge to sin begins with temptation that comes from outside, but that can in no way excuse the sinner. In the New Testament the figure of Satan or the devil emerged as the leader of a metaphysical rebellion against God and as the source of much sin (Luke 11:15; John 12:31; Rev. 12:10). Apart from the work of Christ, the power of sin cannot be broken, but, thanks be to God, for "while we still were sinners Christ died for us" and delivered us from the dominion of sin (Rom. 5:8, 10–11; 6:13–14). And in the end, the devil will be "thrown into the lake of fire and sulfur" (Rev. 20:10; cf. Luke 10:18; Rev. 12:9).

God's Response to Sin

Since sin has such a prominent role in the Bible, it is important to consider God's reaction to this ongoing source of disruption in humankind's relationship with God. What did God do in light of Adam and Eve's disobedience? What was the divine response to the recognition of the human inclination to turn aside from God's way?

In the biblical story, judgment and punishment are God's first responses to human sin. Adam and Eve were expelled from the garden of Eden (Gen. 3:24), and then God unleashed a great flood on the earth (Gen. 7:4). Throughout the Bible God's judgments and punishments are recounted (e.g., Exod. 7:14–12:32; Hos. 4:1–19; Isa. 5:1–7). That is one answer to the question about God's reaction.

But there is another deep current in the Bible that tells of another divine response to the human predicament, namely, the other side of punishment, forgiving grace. Even though God forced Adam and Eve from the garden, God supplied them with protective clothing (Gen. 3:21). While Cain was severely punished for murdering his brother Abel, God put a protective mark on him lest he be killed in retaliation for his misdeed (4:15). Immediately after the great flood, God established a covenant of peace with all humankind, pledging never more to destroy the earth by flood (9:8–17).

God was determined to fashion a positive relationship with humanity. God recognized the difficulty (Gen. 6:5; 8:21) but would not give up the quest. A new approach began with Abraham and Sarah (Gen. 12–22) and continued through Moses (Exod. 1–19, 32–34; Deut. 1–11, 29–34) and David (2 Sam. 7–20). One aspect of the divine approach involved providing ample instruction on how to live beneficially (e.g., Moses and the Torah). Another aspect involved the repeated assurance, given by those called forth by God, of God's continuing determination to establish and maintain relationship with humankind (e.g., the judges, David, and the prophets). Hosea described in powerful language God's refusal to let Israel fall away (Hos. 11:1–9). Isaiah pleaded with his wayward people to repent and return to God, where they would surely find acceptance (Isa. 1:16–20; 55:6–13). At the height of disaster as the Babylonian armies swept in to destroy Judah, the prophet Jeremiah announced that God would establish a new covenant with Israel resting upon divine forgiveness (Jer. 31:13–34).

Of course, the New Testament is the witness to God's all-surpassing action in Jesus Christ to rescue, redeem, and restore God's people in order that the right relationship with God, intended from the beginning, might be established and preserved. In Christ something new is in the process of coming to fulfillment. Perfect purification has been made possible through Jesus' action as heavenly high priest (Heb. 10:1–18). The fullness of Jeremiah's vision is being realized (Heb. 8:1–13). The New Adam has repaired the breach made by the Old Adam (Rom. 5:12–21). Indeed, in Christ God "was reconciling the world to himself, not counting their trespasses against them" (2 Cor. 5:19). There is no illusion that all has been fully completed, but the New Testament is certain that God is committed to overcoming the consequences of sin in order that new life may be found.

Some Concluding Reflections

Sin is indeed an important theme in the Bible. From the Bible's point of view, the human condition is utterly inscrutable apart from the concept of sin. The incapacity or unwillingness of human beings to trust in God's goodness is at the root of all sin. Failure to trust in God leads regularly to trust in human capabilities, sometimes individual but more often social, as in trust or faith in one's race, gender, or nation (i.e., of idolatry).

The consequences of sin are never solely limited to the individual sinner. Disregard for God's way inevitably leads to a disruption of the human community and to an accompanying loss of human dignity, freedom, and possibility. Violent or deceitful acts by individuals foster violent and deceitful actions within and between communities. The commandments give clear direction in how God's people should live. The judgments of God underscore the seriousness with which God takes the matter. Apart from God's repeated willingness to forgive sin, humankind could have little hope. Left completely to their own ends, humans, according to the Bible, would be completely and eternally bogged down in a morass of their own making. But by God's forgiving grace, humankind always has another possibility. Sin is no less serious, but the consequences can be ameliorated, if not eliminated. God does provide repeated chances through the mechanism of forgiveness. Sin has a strong word in the human story, but not the last word. Though humankind was destined to death under the power of sin, thanks to God's grace and mercy the reign of sin has been broken.

Questions for Discussion

1. How is idolatry related to particular sinful actions? Why does the Bible root all sin in the worship of false gods? How is this notion helpful in interpreting sin today?
2. What are the most important breaches in trust today? How do they compare with the types of sin delineated in the Bible and the lists of sinful acts enumerated there? What are the social consequences of these sins today?
3. How does God continue to address the problem of sin? If, as the New Testament says, God has been reconciled with humankind through the life, death, and resurrection of Jesus Christ, what does the continuation of sinful acts by humans mean to God?
4. What should forgiven sinners be doing to demonstrate their forgiveness?

Chapter Five

Law

"I long for your salvation, O Lord, and your law is my delight" (Ps. 119:174). So sings the psalmist toward the end of an extended praise of God and God's law. In so doing, the psalmist alerts the attentive listener to the clear fact that "law" in the Old Testament means much more than simply a legal code. Law, or *torah*, emerges in the history of the First Testament as a central spiritual reality, attributed to Moses and cherished as God's guide into a living relationship with God. There are distinctly legal materials included within *torah*, but the law cannot be reduced to only a collection of statutes.

In 168–167 BCE a man named Mattathias, along with his five sons, initiated a revolt against Greek rule in Palestine with these stirring words: "Let everyone who is zealous for the law and supports the covenant come out with me!" (1 Macc. 2:27). Torah was something revered and worth dying for. The simplistic reduction of *torah* to "Old Testament legalism" over against "New Testament grace" does not do justice to the importance of *torah* in the Bible and in the experience of God's people. The law is rich beyond measure and deserves careful scrutiny.

The Language of the Law

What then are the terms used to articulate the realities included within the law? Among many terms used in reference to various types of laws and regulations, four are used most often in the Old Testament. The first, *mitzvah*, generally translated as "commandment" (Exod. 15:26; Deut. 4:2), refers to specific obligations and instructions. Some indicate things not to be done, while others enjoin things that should be done. (In the New Testament this term is often rendered by *'entole*, "commandment" or "order.") A second term, *dabar*, generally translated "word" or "commandment" (Exod. 34:28; Deut. 10:4), also refers to specific rules or guidelines. The "Ten Commandments" are literally in Hebrew the "Ten Words." A third term, *hoq*, often translated as "statute" or "decree" (Lev. 6:18; Deut. 4:1), seems to refer more to broader principles or policies. The basis for more specific rules is stated as a "statute." (In the New Testament, *prostagma*, "injunction," and *dikaioma*, "regulation," are used to render *hoq*.) The fourth term, *mishpat*, frequently translated "judgment" (Exod. 21:1; Deut. 8:11), denotes ordinances and customs that have been given the status of law. These are judgments that have taken on the status of legal precedents and thereby have become binding.

Though these terms probably each had a distinct connotation in antiquity, it is now often difficult to discriminate the meanings too sharply. Exodus 15:26, where *mitzvah* and *hoq* both occur, and Exodus 24:3, where *dabar* and *mishpat* are used together, may indicate the recognition of a distinction between particular laws in contrast to policylike statements. But all these terms seem to be used almost interchangeably to describe the rich tradition of legal material that has been preserved in the Bible.

There is one more term that is very important in this discussion, *torah*, and it is the only word that is regularly translated into English as "law." This term is very inclusive and connotes much more than the English word "law." In some ways it is unfortunate that *torah* came to be translated "law," but that tradition is too well established to reverse. Sometimes the word *torah* does indicate a particular rule or law (Lev. 6:9, 14), but more often it refers to a broader understanding of the source of all normative instruction, to the whole complex of teaching and experience that the individual "laws" reflect (Exod. 13:9; 16:4). God's "way" or God's "instruction" is a better rendition of *torah* in such contexts.

Such a meaning is reflected in the use of *nomos* in Greek to translate *torah*. *Nomos*, while sometimes referring to particular laws, could be used with reference to the wider, organizing principles of creation and society as determined by God. This broader meaning, though, was clouded when the Latin renderings of the Old and New Testaments used *lex*, "law," with its more particular legal nuance, in translating *nomos*.

What is important to recognize is that *torah* did not originally mean "law" in any narrow, legalistic understanding of that term. *Torah* referred to the guidance and instruction that God provided for Israel. The whole story preserved as Genesis through Deuteronomy came to be called God's *Torah*. That the English word "law" came to be used to identify this rich account is unfortunate. *Torah* is so much more than "rules" or "restrictions."

The Historical Context of the Law

The legal materials preserved in the Old and New Testaments were generated in a historical context. Hundreds of years before the First Testament was written there were collections of laws in Mesopotamia that shaped the emergence of Old Testament law. The code of the Babylonian king Hammurabi, written in the mid-eighteenth century BCE, provides examples of many of the same kinds of laws found in the Old Testament. There are other codes as well, from the Hittites and the Assyrians, that are more contemporary with the biblical materials. Both in style and content there are great similarities among the various collections.

It is not that the biblical materials are directly related literarily with their Mesopotamian counterparts. But the traditions are rooted in the same soil, and some of the same issues arise. Rules governing inheritance, sexual mores, land regulation, family disputes, ritual matters, and much more are preserved and give an insight into the organization and activities within the respective societies. Each of these sources contributes its share to our increasing understanding of the shared historical context.

The collection or codification of the biblical laws seems to have taken place in three main phases, the first around 900 BCE during the period of the monarchy, the second during the middle of the seventh century BCE, and the third in the midst of the Babylonian exile, around the middle of the sixth century BCE. The collections of legal materials were then incorporated into the larger narrative (Genesis–Deuteronomy) toward the end of the exilic period or slightly after the return of the Babylonian exiles to Palestine between 538 and 500 BCE.

The authority of the Torah, the whole collection of materials now known as Genesis through Deuteronomy, began to be acknowledged in the first decades of the fifth century BCE, as reflected in the books of Ezra (Ezra 7:6) and Nehemiah (Neh. 9:3). By the time of Jesus, the "law" (Luke 2:23–24) and the writings of the "prophets" (Luke 16:16) were clearly considered "scripture." During the second and third centuries after the time of Jesus, the term Torah was expanded to include the totality of both the Pentateuch as well as the oral tradition of Moses that served as the basis for the great collection of interpretation preserved in the Talmud. The Torah remains the most authoritative part of the Bible for Jews.

Three Major Collections of Biblical Law

One major collection of biblical laws is called by scholars the "Book of the Covenant." It is preserved as Exodus 20:22–23:33. For the most part, the legal material found here seems to have emerged after Israel settled in the land of Canaan. The Book of the Covenant is probably the oldest collection of laws. While literarily it is set in the narrative of Moses' receiving the Ten Commandments on Mount Sinai (Exod. 20:2–17; Deut. 5:6–21), some of the regulations clearly assume that the people are already in Canaan and are dealing with issues arising in an agricultural setting (Exod. 21:28–32; 22:5–9).

Some of the stipulations in the Book of the Covenant may reflect an earlier format for articulating some of the substance of the Ten Commandments (20:23–26; 21:12–17) and include the penalty for disobedience. At the least, these verses point out a significant difference in the way laws were expressed. Some clearly imply a direct prohibition, like in the Ten Commandments, and are stated as, "Whoever does such and such will be put to death." This type of legal formulation is called "apodictic" or "categorical." It is not totally unique to the biblical tradition, but it is found much more frequently in the Bible than in other Mesopotamian collections. On the other hand, the predominant form of regulation in the Book of the Covenant (and in other parts of the Bible as well) is stated in a "casuistic" or "case law" style—"When such and such happens, then . . ." or, "If such and such, then . . ." (21:18ff.; 21:33ff.)—with formulas for restitution or reconciliation of the problem included.

These early laws probably emerged from the judgments made by the elders of the clans as they adjudicated disputes among their people. This "clan law" also produced the "rules of the talon" (*lex talionis*), which are very limited in number (21:23–25) and have been widely misunderstood. Rather than signs of a barbarian society, these rules were intended to limit the then current practice of retaliation by one family against another when an offense was incurred. Rather than allowing a broad attack of one family for the sake of the honor of its offended member, close regulation was imposed that greatly limited the damage done. (Too often the "eye for an eye, tooth for a tooth" text is taken out of context and used as caricature of Old Testament law as a whole, resulting in the denigration of the Old Testament and its people.)

A second collection of materials is preserved in Deuteronomy 12–26. This material was developed, like that found in the Book of the Covenant, across several centuries. It was gathered and became significant as a "code" during the time of Judah's King

Josiah (ca. 639–609 BCE). After a "book of the law" was discovered during renovations of the temple in 622–621 BCE, the king launched a great reform (2 Kgs. 22:3–23:25). Many scholars believe that Deuteronomy 12–26 forms the core of the book found in the temple.

In style and content the material in Deuteronomy is much like that preserved in Exodus. What is distinctive is the manner in which various adjustments and additions have been made that reflect things that happened in the two hundred or more years between the two collections. There are stipulations limiting the power of kingship (Deut. 17:14–20). A central sanctuary is mandated (12:2–7), and a process for appeal to the Levitical priests and judges is provided (17:8–13). Recognition of the rise of the prophets and ways to judge their authenticity appear (13:1–5; 18:21–22). There are a number of laws intended to curb the misuse and defilement of the land (20:19–20; 21:22–23; 22:9–10; 23:12–14).

Of special importance to this Book of the Law is the prohibition against idolatry of any kind. In the chapters prior to the technical legal materials, numerous warnings against idolatry are recorded (7:5–6, 25–26; 9:8–21; 11:16–17). Within the code, and as part of its summation, the theme was also clearly expressed (12:29–32; 28:14ff.). There is no other god worthy of the people's allegiance. Idolatry will bring spiritual death and the loss of the land. The God of Israel alone is to be worshiped.

The third body of legal material that has been preserved is that which constitutes the book of Leviticus. Many of the laws deal with concerns of ritual propriety, such as the correct forms of sacrifice (Lev. 1–7; 16) and the establishment and ordination of priests (chaps. 8–9). Issues of what is clean and unclean, various purification rites, and the regulation of sexual relations are considered (chaps. 11–19). Because the content deals with so many issues involving cultic and ritual activities, scholars have described this collection as a whole as "priestly."

Within this material is one section that scholars call the "Holiness Code" (chaps. 17–26) because of the repeated use of the term "holy" (e.g., 21:6; 22:2, 32; 25:12; 27:10). This section probably had a separate history as a tradition before being incorporated into its present place in Leviticus. The emphasis within this material is the need for Israel to be different, or set apart, which is the primary meaning of the Hebrew term translated "holy." It was important for the people of Israel to be clearly distinguishable from the peoples among whom they lived. Among the aims of this set of laws are cultic purity, family purity, and singleness of devotion to God. While these instructions may derive from a time earlier than the Babylonian exile, they became especially important to the exiles who were trying to maintain a sense of their identity in the new and strange environment of Babylonia in the middle of the sixth century BCE.

The "Law" in the New Testament

There are at least three rather distinct ways in which "law" is understood within the New Testament. Trying to determine Jesus' own attitude toward the law is difficult given the fact that the Synoptic Gospels were written at least a generation after Jesus' death and resurrection. On the one hand, there is clear evidence that Jesus was remembered as criticizing some of the hypocritical ways that observance of the law was conducted. Jesus seems to have ignored the limitations placed on social relationships with people labeled "tax collectors and sinners" (e.g., Matt. 9:10–11; 11:19; Mark 2:15–16; Luke 7:34; 15:1). Jesus' attitude toward the Sabbath (Mark 2:23–3:6) and his teaching concerning divorce (Matt. 19:2–9; Mark 10:2–12) suggest a willingness to challenge traditional understandings of the law.

On the other hand, the Synoptic Gospels present Jesus as an observer of torah, going regularly to the synagogue on the Sabbath (Mark 1:21; Luke 4:16), teaching there and in the temple (Mark 1:29; 14:49), and acknowledging the legitimacy of such customs as fasting, almsgiving, and prayer (Matt. 5:23–24; 6:1–18). Matthew presents Jesus somewhat as a second Moses who at the beginning of his ministry sets forth a new version of the law (Matt. 5–7). And Matthew remembers Jesus saying, "Do not think that I have come to abolish the law or the prophets; I have come not to abolish but to fulfill" (Matt. 5:17). The critique of the law made by Jesus, much like that of the Old Testament prophets before him, emphasized the moral implications rather than ritualistic obligations. Jesus referred to the Ten Commandments positively (Matt. 19:18–19) and summed up the law, as he understood it, with the twofold admonition to love God and love neighbor (Matt. 22:36–40; Mark 12:30–31; Luke 10:27). Jesus by this view was an observer of the law and commended it to his followers.

A third position was developed by Paul, particularly in Romans and Galatians, and his understanding has led many to an impression that the law was a total burden that enslaved people and led them away from God rather than to God. Paul, or rather Saul of Tarsus, enters the New Testament drama as a fervent observer of and defender of the law, a Pharisee (Phil. 3:5), who vigorously persecuted those who did not follow the law according to his interpretation (Gal. 1:13–14; Phil. 3:4–6; Acts 8:2–3).

After his conversion (Gal. 1:13–24; 2 Cor. 12:1–10; Acts 9:1–18), Paul did a complete about-face. From his new perspective the law seemed to be the agent of condemnation rather than the path to righteousness (Rom. 3:20). Indeed, the law was like a veil that hid the way to God from Paul and any others who sought to observe it (2 Cor. 3:14–15). In contrast to the bondage that Paul experienced under the law, life in Christ was marked by freedom (Gal. 3:23–24; 4:1–7). The law condemned, but Christ came to bring salvation from wrath and death (Rom. 3:19–25; 5:1–11; 7:7–13).

Paul vacillates concerning the place of the law. On the one hand, the law expresses the goodwill of God (Rom. 3:2; 7:12). The law correctly condemns sin (Rom. 2:12; 3:19–20). The law points the way to doing God's will. But at the same time, because of its connection to the "flesh" and "the elemental spirits of the universe," the law is powerless and may even be exploited by demonic forces (Rom. 8:3–7; Gal. 3:19–22; 4:1–11). The greatest difficulty with the way that Paul perceived obedience to the law was that a kind of works righteousness was suggested as being possible. Paul was convinced that justification before God was possible only through faith in Jesus Christ (Rom. 5). There can be no righteousness by any human effort, even the keeping of the law.

For Paul, then, the law played a somewhat positive role in Israel's history in that it prepared the way for the recognition of the grace and forgiveness that God offers in Jesus Christ. But Christ brings the end of the law in that the law reaches its final purpose in Christ (Rom. 8:2). The cross of Christ represented the fulfillment of perfect obedience to God as demanded by the law (Rom. 8:34ff.), and thus for believers, for those "in Christ," removed all obligation to the law. Nonetheless, Paul seems to have developed a conflicted view of the law, sometimes stressing its benefits while at other times viewing it quite negatively (1 Cor. 7:18–20; 8:1–13; Rom. 7:14–25; 8:3–17).

In seeking to understand Paul and relating his view of the law with the way other parts of Scripture suggest, we must consider the time in which he was living. It was a time of great conflict. There was a great struggle going on among Jews and among Christians in terms of self-identity. This may not seem important now, but then neither Judaism nor Christianity had become a religion as such. Each was part of a minority trying to exist with integrity amidst the great religious pluralism of the Roman Empire. Paul was dealing with congregations that were struggling to understand their proper place in the society as a whole and their worth in the eyes of God.

A number of scholars believe that many of Paul's statements about "Jews" were actually directed to Christians who thought they had to copy Jewish patterns in order to please God. These "Judaizers," though they were not born as Jews, insisted that the practice of circumcision be maintained, for instance, and that the observance of the Sabbath and food restrictions of the Jews was necessary if one wanted to be a "true" Christian. These people Paul labeled "Jews" (though they actually were not) and criticized them sharply (Gal. 5:2–6, 11–12; 6:12–13; Phil. 3:2). If this is so, then much of Paul's argument about the law was not directed outward as a critique of actual Jews but was directed inward to the church to assure Christians (Gentile and Jewish converts) that they were as deeply loved by God as the Jews had always been.

Some Concluding Reflections

Torah, the law, is a rich source of guidance, both in its legal contributions as well as its moral instruction. From the Ten Commandments to rules for ritual cleanness, there is much to be learned about the way a society might be ordered to serve the well-being of all. Many of the particular rules may no longer be workable in a modern, urban society. After all, most of us don't have to worry about an ox wandering through our neighborhood and falling in a ditch or goring a neighbor. But caring for one another and making certain that we do not injure others, directly or indirectly, is still important. The law reminds us of our obligations before God and to one another.

The Torah, Genesis though Deuteronomy, also provides numerous accounts of how people successfully and unsuccessfully sought to serve God. From Adam and Eve, Cain and Abel, and Noah, to Abraham and Sarah, Joseph and his brothers, and Moses, from creation to flood to deliverance from slavery in Egypt, it is all found within the Torah, the Law. To ignore this rich treasure trove or to denigrate it, as some Christians seem to do, is a tragedy. Yes, Paul had serious questions about whether the law in itself could bring salvation, but before Paul no one had really claimed that it did. Rather, in the words of the psalmist, the decrees, the precepts, the commandments, the ordinances—that is, the law—are "more to be desired . . . than gold, even much fine gold; sweeter also than honey, and drippings of the honeycomb." What's more, in keeping the law "there is great reward" (Ps. 19:10–11).

Questions for Discussion

1. What are some of the main types of material in the Bible that can be considered under the general category "law"? How do these fit with the meaning of *torah* as "instruction"?

2. How did biblical legal material develop? How did the needs of society influence that development? Does our legal system reflect some of the same methods of creating new laws?
3. How can the great appreciation for torah reflected in Psalm 119 and in most of the Old and New Testaments be squared with the position of Paul? How does each correct and enhance the other?
4. What difference does it make whether Paul was addressing Jews or Judaizers? Do the attitudes of some Christians about the law sometimes result in prejudice and anti-Jewish behavior? If so, should that be changed? How?

Chapter Six

Messiah

The Hebrew word *mashach*, upon which the English "messiah" is based, means to "smear" or to "pour" oil or ointment on something or someone. The action being described can be as formal as pouring oil on the head of someone for the purpose of ritually anointing, or as informal as simply applying ointment to the body after bathing. After oil has been applied to someone or something, using the term in its adjectival or its participial form indicates that the object that was "smeared" was thereby "anointed." In some instances, particularly when used of a person, the translation "the anointed one" or simply "the messiah" is appropriate.

"Messiah" is found in both the First and the Second Testaments, but it is far more frequent in the Second, where it appears in Greek as "Christ." Because "Messiah" or "Christ" take on special meaning when applied to Jesus of Nazareth, it is important to review the use of the terms in both testaments as well as to consider some of the changes that took place in the several hundred years between the testaments. Old Testament usage is foundational, but the New Testament and extrabiblical writings of the first century are most instructive for understanding the development of the meaning of the term "Messiah."

Basic Old Testament Meanings

When the first child born to Bathsheba and David became ill, David fasted and prayed in hopes that the child would live. But after the child died, David rose, washed and anointed himself (i.e., put oil on himself), and got dressed (2 Sam. 12:20). Amos chastised the rich for anointing themselves with the finest oils, that is, for their extravagant use of bath oils in the face of extreme poverty among the common folk (Amos 6:6). The psalmist, reflecting on the practices of hospitality common in the ancient Near East, acknowledged the graciousness of the host who anoints the guest with fine oil (Ps. 23:5).

Far more frequent than these examples, however, is the more formal use of the term *mashach* to describe the ritual of setting apart space or equipment for the worship of God or for the setting apart, the "ordaining," of human personnel for special service as priests or kings. First, consider the anointing of things and people associated directly with the worship of God. In an elaborate ceremony, Aaron and his sons were set aside for special service before God at the sanctuary (Exod. 28:40–29:9). Special garments were prepared, and special oil was poured on Aaron's head as an act of consecration (Exod. 30:30; Ps. 133:2). Indeed, the special oil was also used to anoint and thereby consecrate "the tent of meeting and the ark of the covenant, and the table and all its utensils, and the lampstand and its utensils, and the altar of incense, and the altar of burnt offering with all its utensils, and the basin with its stand" (Exod. 30:26–28; cf. 40:1–33; Lev. 8:10–12). Special wafers "spread with oil" (i.e., "smeared" or "anointed" with oil) are also mentioned (Exod. 29:2; Lev. 2:4).

Later, as the priesthood developed, one priest was elevated among his peers. This "high priest" was set apart in a special ceremony much like that first enjoined for Aaron. Special instructions were given for "the priest who is exalted above his fellows, on whose head the anointing oil has been poured" (Lev. 21:10–15). And, in the case of ritual defilement, special purification rites are prescribed for this one who is called "the anointed priest" (Lev. 4:2–21). When *mashach* and its related grammatical forms appear in Exodus, Leviticus, and Numbers, they are almost exclusively used in reference to activities related to priests or consecrated places and their furnishings.

In the books of Judges, 1 and 2 Samuel, 1 and 2 Kings, and Psalms, however, the primary referent of *mashach* is a king. As part of the selection and induction process, the person selected to be king was "anointed" with oil, usually by a prophet. This grew from the fact that when Israel first demanded the institution of kingship, God sent Samuel to anoint first Saul and then David to designate them as king (cf. 1 Sam. 10:1; 16:12–13). Thus, so long as the monarchy existed, the king, whose authority was completely dependent upon the empowering of God, was called "the Lord's anointed," "his anointed," and "my anointed" (e.g., 1 Sam. 2:10, 35; 12:3, 5; 24:6, 10; Ps. 2:2; 18:50; 132:17). In the history of kingship in Israel, Saul (ca. 1020–1000 BCE) is often considered the first king. But about a century earlier, a fellow named Abimelech had persuaded the elders of Shechem and Beth-millo to declare him king. But this effort to establish a monarchy was not authorized by God, according to the tradition, and Abimelech was not "anointed" by a representative of the Lord (Judg. 9:1–6). Thus, he was not recognized as, or called, "the Lord's anointed" in the tradition.

Samuel, one of the "judges" and thereby recognized as God's designated spokesman at the time, at first strongly opposed the inauguration of kingship (1 Sam. 8–12). He considered the effort to do so by the people as a criticism of his own work as judge and as a denial of God's authority. For the previous two hundred years or so, God alone had been considered "king" of God's people. If necessary, God would at times designate a person as a "judge" for a special role, usually to lead the fight against an enemy who had oppressed or threatened to oppress God's people. Among those set aside by God to be these so-called judges were individuals such as Deborah, Gideon, and Samuel. Thus, even when judges exercised authority over the people, this was not understood as compromising the long-standing tradition that God alone was king. The power of this conviction is seen in that even after the Davidic monarchy was finally established, some psalms written years later (e.g., Pss. 93, 97, and 99) began with the declaration that "the Lord is king!" Only the Lord God can be proclaimed the king of glory (Ps. 24:8).

Only over Samuel's strenuous protests were Saul and later David chosen as kings over Israel. They were each anointed by Samuel with oil at God's direction (1 Sam. 10:1; 16:13) and thereby became "the Lord's anointed," "messiahs," in the service of God. The kings of Israel and Judah were never deified or perceived as gods as was often the case among the surrounding peoples. At times some extravagant language, language that made it sound as if the king were godlike, was used in praise of the king (Pss. 2:7–9; 45:1, 6–7; Isa. 9:6), but in light of the whole tradition it is clear that kings were always recognized as mortals. The king might be a special representative of God, but the support of kingship in general, and of any individual king in particular, was always qualified in light of the instructions of Deuteronomy 17:14–20 and the ever-present critique of the prophets.

Nonetheless, a strong tradition developed concerning David that God had chosen him to be king and had promised that one of his offspring would occupy the throne "forever" (2 Sam. 7:8–16). Nathan the prophet delivered this announcement to David, and subsequently each "son of David," each new king of Judah, was anointed as king at the appropriate time (1 Kgs. 1:39). The Davidic dynasty was established. Each "son of David" was "adopted" ritually as God's "son" (2 Sam. 7:14; Pss. 2:7; 89:26–27). In this sense, each king in David's line was understood to be God's anointed.

Being messiah, then, according to this view, meant being chosen and installed in obedience to God for the service of God. Even a foreign king, the great King Cyrus of Persia, could be said to be God's messiah (Isa. 45:1) because Cyrus responded to God's bidding to come to Israel's relief and break the bondage of Babylon. What's more, Cyrus was described with an additional royal title, "shepherd," as acknowledgment of his service to God (Isa. 44:28).

For some four hundred years, a "son of David" sat on the throne of Judah, giving persuasive witness to the power of God's promise. But there were many times when the reign of a particular king was marked by deceit, by disobedience to God's way, by oppression by foreign powers, and the like. In these instances, God's "anointed" at best seemed ineffective and at worst seemed a mockery of the title "messiah." Any positive content of the title seemed lost.

Some people, particularly some prophets, began to look ahead to a time when a more perfect king, a more obedient messiah, and a more Godlike kingdom might be established. Isaiah, for instance, glimpsed a day when a new king would appear who would be called "Wonderful Counselor, Mighty God, Everlasting Father, Prince of Peace" and would establish justice with righteousness (Isa. 9:2–7). A peaceable, just kingdom on earth would be established by a "shoot" from the "stump of Jesse," empowered by the spirit of God (Isa. 11:1–9). In actual historical terms, in terms of human ability, such possibilities seemed remote, but across the years these hopes came to form a basic desire for a messiah or a "messianic age" that was important at least to some of God's people.

Between the Testaments

Much took place in the social, political, and religious world of the Jews between 200 BCE and the time of Jesus that had a significant impact on the understanding of "the messiah." While there was a brief period of autonomy after the Maccabean Revolt (167–164 BCE) against Antiochus IV Epiphanes, the Seleucid king of Syria who instituted a harsh program of Hellenization in Judea, the monarchy and David's dynasty were long gone. The high priest was certainly one who was anointed, but priestly anointing did not carry the same connotation that had attached to the consecration of the kings. The high priest simply was not thought of as the Lord's anointed in the way the kings had been. "Messiah," as a title, was a royal term, not a priestly one.

The religious and political setting in Judea was marked by diversity rather than unity. There was no one group or party that could unquestionably speak for all the Jews. Because Judaism as an organized religion did not emerge until the second century CE, in parallel with the emergence of Christianity, it is not possible to assert with any certainty "what the Jews believed" in the first century. Different groups held a variety of views on many topics, including the role of and importance of the messiah.

Among the general population, however, interest in the messiah was practically nonexistent. Though many Christians have believed and continue to believe that Jesus' contemporaries were desperately awaiting a deliverer, the Messiah of God, who would free them (militarily if necessary) from the tyranny of Rome, there is little evidence to support this view. Active hope for a "messianic age" was also marginal. To be sure, some did interpret some of the references in the prophets as pointing to a messiah to come, but these writers by no means represented a majority. Further, there were some who were willing to risk armed conflict in their conviction that God would intervene and deliver them from their oppressors to bring a glorious age, a messianic kingdom, but again, these were far from representative of the people as a whole.

It does seem fairly clear that by the time of Jesus, the Pharisees were the largest single party among a number of groups (e.g., Sadducees, Zealots) that existed. Pharisaism, so far as can be determined, did not encourage hopes for a messiah. From the Pharisees' point of view, the political option of autonomy from Rome that was implicit in royal messianic language was not possible. Indeed, it was dangerous, as several semi-revolts had demonstrated. Thus, the Pharisees had shifted the emphasis away from any "this worldly" expectations concerning the establishment of God's peaceable kingdom. They taught, rather, a hope based upon the resurrection of individuals from the dead and on rewards and punishments to be experienced beyond this world in an "other worldly" sphere. In their system of theology there was simply no need or expectation of a messiah.

To defend their position, the Pharisees across the years developed several criteria to use in determining the legitimacy of the claims of anyone to be the messiah. These included the need for the person to demonstrate undisputed descent from King David, to perform clear signs and wonders, to be preceded by the return of Elijah, and to achieve the establishment of the messianic kingdom as described by some of the prophets. The Pharisees considered these conditions impossible to meet and thus, ipso facto, the claim of anyone to be the messiah was automatically disqualified.

Messiah in the New Testament

The first thing that should be noted when turning to the New Testament is that the Greek language did not really have an appropriate equivalent for "anointed one." The Greek verb *chrio*, chosen to render *mashach*, meant "to smear" or "to rub." While in Hebrew the adjectival or participial forms of the verb were understandable, the Greek translation, *christos*, came out sounding rather strange to the uninitiated. It literally meant "the smeared one"—not exactly an inviting image. By the end of the first century CE, in fact, because of the way it was used, *christos*, rather than being a title, became for many the equivalent of a proper name with little, if any, messianic content.

This is evident already in the writings of Paul. In 1 Corinthians 15:3 Paul wrote "that Christ died for our sins in accordance with the scriptures," using *christos*, for all practical purposes, as a proper name. Similar examples are numerous, this being the primary way that Paul employed the term (e.g., Rom. 1:6; 5:6; 1 Cor. 1:6, 17). In a very few places, Paul placed the definite article "the" before *christos*, indicating a title rather than a name (e.g., Rom. 9:5). But most of the time, as indicated by the special phrase so characteristic of Paul's thought—being "in Christ"—*christos* seems to have little, if any, connection with messianic expectations as commonly understood.

How much of the original royal content of the term was operative in Paul's thought is difficult to determine. Certainly it is

"Christ" who will come again in some of Paul's eschatological announcements (1 Thess. 2:19; 3:13; 4:15–16; 5:23), but it is not at all clear whether Paul envisaged Jesus' return as involving a role as "king of an earthly kingdom" as in some of the messianic hopes that had developed across the centuries. Perhaps Paul used *christos* as he did simply because few of his Gentile converts would have understood the nuance of the Jewish term "messiah." Whatever the case, in most places, Paul appears to have used either "Christ" or "Jesus Christ" or "Christ Jesus" simply as the name of the one he knew as Lord.

The Gospels, on the other hand, regularly refer to Jesus as "the Christ." While Mark uses *christos* as a name twice (Mark 1:1; 9:41), elsewhere the term appears with the definite article as a title. In Matthew and Luke the translation "the Messiah" seems always to be appropriate. Such is the case in John as well, with the exception of two places where *messias* (a Greek transliteration of *machach*) appears apparently as a name (John 1:41; 4:25) and in two other texts where "Jesus Christ" appears (John 1:17; 17:3).

Though Matthew and Luke each supply a genealogy of Jesus that relates him to the lineage of David (Matt. 1:1–17; Luke 3:23–38), more important was Jesus' interpretation of Psalm 110:1 challenging the claim of the Pharisees that the first essential mark of the messiah was that he had to be the "son of David" (Matt. 22:41–46; Mark 12:35–37; Luke 20:41–44). Further, Matthew and Luke refined the role of the messiah, emphasizing his teaching (Matt. 7:28–29; 8:19; 23:10) and his suffering (Luke 9:22, 43–45; 12:50; 13:32–33; 17:25; 18:31–34; 24:26, 46). On this latter point, Isaiah 53 had deepened the notion of who the messiah was and what the messianic role involved.

The Gospel of John contains an interesting passage where the works of Jesus and the origin of Jesus were debated among the people and the Pharisees. Jesus' brothers challenged him to go to Jerusalem and demonstrate his power so that all could see what he was doing (John 7:3–5). Jesus declined initially but then went to Jerusalem and taught in the temple (7:14–18). The authorities were amazed at Jesus' knowledge and ability (7:15). Jesus also performed acts of healing that stirred up the crowds, some in anger because he healed on the Sabbath and some in astonishment at the power he demonstrated (7:19–24, 31). Some wondered whether Jesus was the messiah and questioned whether the authorities in fact knew this but sought to keep it secret (7:25–26). The scene ended with the Pharisees "settling the question" by challenging anyone to show where the scriptures suggested that the messiah could possibly come out of Galilee, the place from which Jesus had most obviously come (7:41, 52). This long discourse demonstrates, among other things, how Christian writers at the end of the first century CE, when it is believed that the Gospel of John was written, were actively engaged in challenging the generally accepted views of the Pharisees regarding the coming of the messiah.

Whether Jesus himself thought of himself as the messiah is difficult to determine. On the one hand, he seems to have resisted any notion of armed resistance against the authorities (Matt. 5:39–41; 26:51–55; John 18:10), a position that seems unlikely if he considered himself a political figure in the mode of messiah. But on the other hand, the Gospels are unanimous in reporting that the charge the Roman authorities posted on Jesus' cross was a political one, namely, that he was "the King of the Jews" (Matt. 27:37; Mark 15:26; Luke 23:38; John 19:19). This suggests that Jesus, or at least some of his contemporaries (followers and/or enemies), did indeed consider him to be the messiah.

If Jesus did embrace the idea of being the messiah, it was certainly not in the political sense that was implicit in the early monarchial understanding of being "the Lord's anointed." The Spirit of God was upon Jesus, and this was the "anointing" he deserved and received. Jesus was "the Son of God," a royal, messianic designation, but his kingdom was not of this world (John 18:36). So far as the New Testament was concerned, Jesus was clearly the messiah, but the meaning of that term was radically transformed in light of the life, death, and resurrection of the Lord, and the messianic age to come was understood to be outside the realm of history as such. Nonetheless, by the very use of a political term like "messiah," an important claim was made that the lordship of Jesus engaged the whole of life, "spiritual" and otherwise.

Some Concluding Reflections

In its origins, "messiah" was a functional term, describing the pouring of oil on the head of a person as an act of consecration. The person was thereby set apart for special service, perhaps as a priest or more often as a king. Such anointing was common among ancient Semitic peoples, but it was not practiced to the same degree among the Greeks or the Romans.

Through the course of time the term took on special meaning because of its use to designate those of David's dynasty. David's "sons" were each a "messiah." As the monarchy declined and eventually ceased to exist, the promise of God to David assuring the perpetuity of David's "house" was projected into the future. An ideal king along the lines of the prophetic teachings was hoped for. God's reign continued to have a very real earthly side even when it was idealized.

In the New Testament the title of "Messiah" was claimed for Jesus. In this process the meaning of the term was changed in significant ways, particularly with regard to the way Jesus the Messiah was understood as teacher and as sufferer. Though the apologists of the early church possibly misrepresented the ideas of their contemporaries in their zeal to testify to Jesus, the witness that he was the Messiah was important, among other reasons, because it implicitly affirmed that Jesus' work was "worldly" even as it was "spiritual."

Questions for Discussion

1. How does knowledge about the origin of the term "messiah" help you understand the implications of the church's claim that Jesus is the Messiah?
2. What difference does it make that most of the Jews at the

time of Jesus were not, in fact, looking for or expecting the coming of a messiah?

3. What is really important about assigning the title "Messiah" to Jesus? In what ways does that influence the way Jesus is presented? How did the New Testament maintain and redefine the term as it was used in the Old Testament?

4. How have Christians at times misrepresented the Pharisees? How is the Pharisees' teaching about the coming messiah similar to and different from what many Christians believe today about the "second coming" of the Lord?

Chapter Seven

Spirit

The English word "spirit" can be used in reference to many things. One can have "school spirit," dedication and enthusiasm for an educational institution. One can "show spirit" by being willing to try new things or wrestle with difficult matters. One is in "good spirits" when one expresses joy and happiness. One can seek to understand the "spirit of the times" amidst the many currents blowing across the world.

One can also use the term to refer to the inner being of God or of a human. Human beings were given "breath" or "spirit" by God and were thus animated into life. In Greek culture the "human spirit" was deemed immortal and constituted the essence of the individual. That is a widely accepted understanding of the term today. It is used as a synonym for "soul." As discussed in chapter 3, however, there is more to the issue than is generally assumed. The reader should review the material there with respect to the meaning of the term as related to humankind. In this chapter the concentration will be on God's Spirit and how that is understood in the Bible.

Spirit as Divine Agent

There is a basic ambiguity in the "spirit language" that the opening verses of Genesis reveal well. As the NRSV translates, "a wind from God swept over the face of the waters" (Gen. 1:2; cf. 8:1). But the verse can also be translated as in the NIV: "The Spirit of God was hovering over the waters." How is the Hebrew word *ruah* to be translated? Should it be "wind," the movement of air (Gen. 3:8), or "spirit," referring to something immaterial within God by which God directs, empowers, and otherwise relates to the world, and to human beings in particular? Should the English translation be capitalized or not? Is there a difference between "spirit," "Spirit, " and "Holy Spirit," all of which appear in various places in English translations? The Hebrew term *ruah* is feminine in gender, while the Greek term *pneuma* is neuter. What, if anything, should be made of such linguistic data? These are some of the issues and the poles between which interpretation is to be made.

The same ambiguity with the Greek word *pneuma* allows for a beautiful wordplay in the Gospel of John. Jesus instructed Nicodemus, a Pharisee and a "leader of the Jews" (John 3:1), saying; "The wind [*pneuma* = spirit?] blows where it chooses, and you hear the sound of it, but you do not know where it comes from or where it goes. So it is with everyone who is born of the Spirit [*pneuma* = wind?]" (3:8). Verse 6 has Jesus saying, "What is born of flesh is flesh, and what is born of the Spirit [*pneuma*] is spirit [*pneuma*]." Neither *pneuma* is capitalized in the Greek. The decision to render the first term "Spirit" in the NRSV is a translator's choice that may convey a more personalized understanding of *pneuma* than was intended by the author of the Gospel. The original Greek text is a little more ambiguous.

In many places in the Bible, *ruah* or *pneuma* are used to describe actions of God where "wind" is the agent. For instance, in Exodus God brings a plague of locusts upon Egypt by the agency of an "east wind" (Exod. 10:13, 19). Likewise, God, using the "east wind," divided the waters of the Reed Sea (Exod. 14:21), that "wind" being described poetically as "a blast of your [God's] nostrils" (Exod. 15:8, 10). The prophet Jonah was thwarted in his flight from doing God's will when God "hurled a great wind upon the sea" (Jonah 1:4). Jeremiah declared that "a hot wind . . . out of the bare heights in the desert" was the agent of divine judgment (Jer. 4:11). God's coming to Adam and Eve was "at the time of the evening breeze" (Gen. 3:8). Poetically, the wind was viewed as a vehicle for God's transport (Ps. 104:3–4; cf. 2 Sam. 22:16). God's appearances were often accompanied by storm clouds and wind, and acts of divine deliverance were enabled by the power of God's breath (Ps. 18:15–20; Ezek. 1:4). The creative acts of God are attributed equally to the divine "word" and the "breath" of God's mouth (Ps. 33:6). What is important to remember is that almost every time *ruah* and *pneuma* are encountered in the biblical text, the dual possibility in translation (wind/spirit) is possible.

Spirit as Divine Inspiration

The divine "spirit" was also believed to be the source of what is now called "inspiration." This might take the form of artistic talent (see Exod. 28:3, where the Hebrew for "endowed with skill" in the NRSV is literally "a skilled/wise *ruah*"). Bezalel son of Uri son of Hur was noted because God "filled him with divine spirit, with ability, intelligence, and knowledge in every kind of craft" (Exod. 31:3). Moses was directed in his administrative work by God's spirit, a spirit that could also be shared with others (Num. 11:17, 25–29).

God also poured out breath or spirit on individuals who in turn prophesied (Num. 24:2; 2 Sam. 23:2–3; 2 Chron. 15:1; 20:14; 24:20). These persons were "inspired" by the divine spirit. Such behavior could be viewed quite positively (Isa. 61:1). But sometimes, particularly when prophesying was accompanied by ecstatic behavior, questions were raised (1 Sam. 10:5–11). Did the divine spirit actually lead to irrational seizures? Further, there were some prophets who were charged with uttering false prophecies (Jer. 28:15–16; 29:21–23). Indeed, some believed that lying, deceiving, or evil spirits could, in fact, also be sent by God to unsettle individuals or produce false prophecies (1 Sam. 16:15–16; 1 Kgs. 22:20–23). Nonetheless, a basically positive hope persisted that God in the end-time would bless humankind by pouring "spirit" upon all flesh, enabling a renewal of prophecy (Joel 2:28–29; cf. Acts 2:17–21).

It is important to note that "inspiration gone wrong" created a serious theological problem. How was evil related to the power of the divine spirit? Was God indeed responsible for lying spirits, as some Old Testament passages suggested? During New Testament times the tradition of lying spirits fit easily into a widespread belief in demons. In a culture where many gods and goddesses were acknowledged, it was not difficult to imagine a large number of lesser deities who, while they could bring blessing, largely brought pain and discomfort to individuals and to communities.

In the Gospel of Mark, Jesus is remembered as encountering a man possessed and tormented by demons (Mark 5:1–5). He exorcised the demons from the man and allowed them to possess a herd of swine that then rushed into the Sea of Galilee (5:6–13). In significant other passages Jesus dealt with a variety of demons that plagued the people and sometimes resisted him (Mark 1:21–28; 3:22–27; 7:24–30; 9:14–29; Matt. 12:22–32; Luke 11:14–23).

For the apostle Paul, these evil spirits or demons were addressed under the language of "principalities" and "powers" (Rom. 8:38; 1 Cor. 10:20; Col. 1:16; 2:15). Though finally they would be subdued by the power of God in Christ, until that time they worked evil in the world and were to be resisted. In the Gospel of John, on the other hand, there are no exorcisms. While Jesus was accused of being under the influence of demons (John 7:20; 8:48–49; 10:20–21), the Gospel clearly understood the devil to be the one who instigated evil action (John 13:2). Evil was in a sense concentrated in one figure.

The Bible does not explain how these evil powers came into existence. Extrabiblical sources tell of a rebellion by some of the angels in heaven against God and the subsequent expulsion of the leader, the devil, for this disobedience (*1 En.* 6:1–19:3; 54:6; 69:5; cf. Jude 6; 2 Pet. 2:4; Rev. 12:9). But however the tradition arose, the archfiend was known under a number of designations, such as Belial, Beliar, Mastemah, and Beelzebub. Besides these names, in the New Testament the devil is also called the "tempter" (Matt. 4:3), "the ruler of the demons" (Luke 11:15), and "the ruler of this world" (John 12:31). The Bible resisted any form of absolute dualism. Thus, the evil spirits were recognized as real but not envisioned in any way as an ultimate threat against the sovereignty of God.

Spirit as Divine Empowerment

While inspiration was certainly a form of empowerment, there is another sphere of activity to which the term can be applied. The Davidic rulers were considered especially in need of the spirit of God for empowerment to rule wisely and make righteous judgments (Isa. 11:1–5). Israel as a people was gifted with the divine spirit to bring God's justice to the nations (Isa. 42:1; 44:3; 59:21; 61:1). By God's spirit Joseph was enabled to interpret Pharaoh's dream (Gen. 41:38). Othniel, Gideon, and Samson, all considered "judges" in Israel's tradition, were empowered by the divine spirit (Judg. 3:10; 6:34; 14:6, 19; 15:14). Saul, by God's spirit, rallied his people to resist the Ammonites (1 Sam. 11:5–11).

In the Second Testament there is considerable attention given to the manner in which God's spirit affects the way God's people deal with one another and how they live in the world. Paul particularly uses the metaphor of "spiritual fruit" to illustrate the difference he believed should be evident among those who followed Jesus (Gal. 5:22–26; cf. Matt. 7:16–18; Luke 6:43–45). By the empowerment of God's spirit, humans can be changed and enabled to love one another with compassion and forgiveness, fully, as God intends (Gal. 5:13–15; cf. Rom. 15:30; 1 Cor. 13:13–14:1; Eph. 3:16–17; 4:3–4, 30–32; Phil. 2:1). Relationships between people are affected by God's spirit, and as a consequence the quality of life in the community of the church is improved.

In Acts the empowerment of the church is directly connected to the power of God's spirit. The first empowerment is described dramatically: "And suddenly from heaven there came a sound like the rush of a violent wind, and it filled the entire house where they were sitting. Divided tongues, as of fire, appeared among them, and a tongue rested on each of them" (Acts 2:2–3). There followed prophetic speech in "other languages, as the Spirit gave them ability" (2:4; cf. the ecstatic language that required interpreters, described by Paul in 1 Cor. 14:1–25), which witnessed to "God's deeds of power" (2:11). The event was understood as a fulfillment of Joel's prophecy of an outpouring of God's spirit (2:16–21; Joel 2:28–32; cf. Ezek. 11:19; 36:27). The nearness of the eschatological kingdom of God was thereby attested. The coming of the spirit was, as Paul put it, the "first installment" God made in the establishment of that reign (2 Cor. 1:22).

As the story of the early church unfolds in Acts following this event, the empowerment by the spirit is evidenced in numerous ways. Peter was enabled to preach powerfully (Acts 2:22–36; 3:11–26; 4:8–12), to heal (3:1–10), to raise the dead (9:32–43), to proclaim the gospel to Gentiles who in turn received empowerment by the spirit (10:1–48). Stephen and Barnabas are also described as especially empowered by the spirit for ministry (6:3–5; 7:55; 11:24). The community as a whole responded by gathering frequently for prayer (4:23–31) and by sharing their possessions (4:32–37). The marvel was that "uneducated and ordinary" people (4:13) became dynamic witnesses to the power of God to transform individuals and communities.

One additional empowerment is important to consider, namely, that of Jesus of Nazareth. Each of the Gospels report that God's spirit came upon Jesus at his baptism by John in the Jordan River (Matt. 3:13–17; Mark 1:9–11; Luke 3:21–22; John 1:29–34). All attest that the spirit "descended like a dove" to rest on Jesus, accompanied by the announcement that Jesus was the Son of God. The image of a dove as the symbol of God's spirit is unique to the baptism of Jesus. Perhaps it is an echo of the Noah story where a dove becomes the agent by which the end of the flood is recognized (Gen. 8:8–12).

For each of the Gospel writers, this account provides the beginning point for Jesus' ministry and an "explanation" of Jesus' extraordinary relationship with God. Indeed, Luke boldly attests that in Jesus the very fulfillment of Isaiah's word is realized: "The Spirit of the Lord is upon me, because he has anointed me to bring good news to the poor. He has sent me to proclaim release to the captives and recovery of sight to the blind, to let the oppressed go free, to proclaim the year of the Lord's favor" (Luke 4:18–19; Isa. 61:1–2). As with Israel and then with the church, the power of the divine spirit enabled Jesus to do what he was intended to do. Why Jesus would need to be so empowered, however, raises a question about Jesus' relationship with God. This concern eventually led the church to develop the doctrine of the Trinity.

Spirit as Divine Presence

Thus far, examples of the manifestation of God's spirit within human community and by individual humans have been the main focus. But there are many places where spirit language is used primarily to express a sense of the divine presence. God is, after all, immaterial, invisible so far as the human eye is concerned but, though invisible, is often quite near. "To whom then will you liken God," the prophet asked. What visible image can be compared with the incomparable God of Israel (Isa. 40:18–26)? None!

The making of idols and images has always been a means by which humans have tried to symbolize and ensure divine presence. In the Bible such efforts are ridiculed and denounced. Isaiah scorns those who fashion a "god" out of one end of a log while warming themselves and cooking over the other end (Isa. 44:12–20). Jeremiah also mocks such efforts (Jer. 10:1–9) and finally, and simply, sums up the inadequacy of idols with the statement, "There is no breath [*ruah*] in them" (10:14). Israel was expressly forbidden to fashion any kind of idol or to bow down to any such human construction (Exod. 20:4–5; Deut. 4:15–20; 5:8–9). Rather, the presence of the invisible God was believed enthroned over the ark of the covenant, first in the tabernacle and then in the Holy of Holies in Solomon's temple.

Spirit language is one of the ways God's presence was expressed. As the psalmist put it: "Where can I go from your spirit? Or where can I flee from your presence?" (Ps. 139:7). Or again, "Do not cast me away from your presence, and do not take your holy spirit from me" (Ps. 51:11). The "face" (translated "presence" in the NRSV) of God (Exod. 33:14–15), the "glory" of God (Exod. 40:34–38), and the "name" of God (Deut. 12:5, 11, 21; 14:23–24) were terms also used to express the conviction that God was present and available to those who would turn to God. God was near, not far (Isa. 55:6).

The apostle Paul brought the realization of the nearness of the divine presence to its peak by declaring that the spirit of God, the spirit of Christ, dwelt among the people within the church (Rom. 8:9). Isaiah had intimated the same thing in his symbolic use of the term *Immanuel*, "God with us," but it had a negative connotation there (Isa. 8:5–10). For Paul, however, the emphasis was positive. As the spirit was not flesh, so God's people were no longer enslaved by flesh (Rom. 8:5–8). In the power of God's presence, in God's spirit, the church waits, with all the rest of creation, for the freedom God has promised (8:19–25). The spirit and God are so closely identified that every need of God's people is known (8:26–27). Indeed, God's spirit, God's presence, and the love of Christ are so closely intertwined that Paul can boldly proclaim that nothing can "separate us from the love of God in Christ Jesus our Lord" (8:39).

Spirit as Divine Person

Thus far, God's spirit has been considered apart from the person-hood of God, but such a separation does not reflect the deep understanding within the Bible that God is in fact spirit (John 4:24). God's very person is best understood as spirit, and indeed, as Holy Spirit. There are numerous places in the Bible, especially in the New Testament, where the action and presence of the Holy Spirit is understood as the direct action and presence of God (cf. Luke 3:22; 12:12; Acts 4:31; 5:32; 10:44; 15:28; 1 Cor. 6:19; Eph. 4:30).

The question arises however as to whether "spirit" can in any way be understood as a separate entity distinct from God. "Wisdom" was apparently so considered (Prov. 8:22–36). In Isaiah there are two passages that may be construed as using "spirit" as somewhat independent from God. In Isaiah 48:16, God's spirit seems to be differentiated from God and is sent to accompany the prophet in addressing the people, but the reader is left with the impression that the presence of God's very person is what is being emphasized. In Isaiah 63:10, the disobedience of the people "grieved his [God's] holy spirit" and resulted in God's withdrawing the divine presence (Isa. 63:11). For God's presence to be among the people, for God's spirit to stand in their midst, meant that God was personally present in a powerful way (Hag. 2:5; Zech. 4:6). But this could be expressed by language that distinguished between God and God's spirit.

In the New Testament, the fact that Jesus was remembered as receiving the Spirit at his baptism (e.g., Mark 1:10) and praying to God the Father (e.g., Mark 14:36), for instance, suggested language that reflected this distinctiveness between Father, Jesus, and Spirit (2 Cor. 13:13; Eph. 4:4–6). In the Gospel of John the appearance of the Advocate, the Spirit of Truth (i.e., the Paraclete), promised by Jesus, seems to advance this same differentiation (John 14:16–17; 16:13–15). The Paraclete seems separate from both God and Jesus, being sent by God and functioning in Jesus' place after Jesus "goes away" (John 14:16; 16:7–11). Because the Greek term *paracletos* is masculine in gender, a personal tone was introduced into the text that perhaps wrongly emphasized a personal character to the Paraclete that was actually unwarranted. Nonetheless, the references to the Paraclete heighten the ambiguity of the imagery in that, while the Paraclete is identified with the Spirit (14:26), the Paraclete is also called the "Spirit of truth" somehow seemingly to be distinguished from the Holy Spirit (15:26; 16:13). What's more, for John, there was a time before which (7:39) and after which (20:22) the Holy Spirit came to the community of believers.

One further passage should be noted. Matthew instructs baptism to be done "in the name of the Father and of the Son and of the Holy Spirit" (Matt. 28:19). This formula seems clearly to posit the three named as separate, though indivisibly related (cf. Rom. 15:30; 1 Pet. 1:2; Jude 20). But Matthew nonetheless remained within the monotheistic tradition rooted in the Hebrew Bible (Matt. 12:28; 22:43).

Though Matthew (as did other New Testament writers) utilized a threefold pattern, his was not the technical trinitarian language that would be developed some three hundred years later. There was no effort to describe how each "person" was related to the other or whether each was coeternal or of the same substance. The trinitarian "solution" as to how the immaterial Creator of the world could be present in the person of a specific, particular human being, namely, Jesus of Nazareth, certainly built on spirit language, but it went places that the Bible had not gone.

Some Concluding Reflections

The place and work of the Spirit is well attested in the Bible. Spirit language serves well to express the immateriality of God and the absolute freedom of God. By the Spirit, God initiates all manner of activity by individuals and within human communities. By the Spirit, God's presence is made known, God's will is expressed, and God's deliverance and judgment are realized. On the one hand, God's movements and actions may use the agency of the "wind." On the other hand, the Spirit remains invisible and totally "other" and distinct from the created order. God and Spirit are deeply connected and yet separate in the experience of God's people.

The central function of spirit language was to make clear to God's people that God was always present and prepared to act. God would not leave the people alone or without guidance. Before the coming of Jesus and after Jesus' incarnation, resurrection, and ascension, God's spirit was actively assisting in bringing God's reign to realization. The Spirit was both separable and inseparable from God and from Jesus. Most often the Spirit was identified as God's spirit or Christ's spirit, but this did not lessen its significance or power. It is still the case that "God is spirit, and those who worship him must worship in spirit and truth" (John 4:24).

Questions for Discussion

1. How does the knowledge that spirit language can be used for "wind" or "breath," as well as for "invisible spirit," enrich interpretation?
2. What are some of the ways that God's spirit inspires and empowers people today? Are there still prophets or not? Why or why not?
3. How are the presence and absence of God related to the spirit of God?
4. What difference does it make that "spirit" in the language of the Bible is either feminine (Hebrew) or neuter (Greek)? Should contemporary interpretation reflect this? Why or why not?

Chapter Eight

Grace

There are two terms in the Bible, one Hebrew and the other Greek, regularly translated as "grace" or "favor." Both of these terms were used commonly in the cultures of the day. The Hebrew noun *hen* (or the adjective *hannun*) refers to a favor sought or granted or to a quality in a person that can be described as pleasant or gracious. There is a wider set of terms used for making supplication, for pleading before God, associated with these Hebrew terms. The Greek word *charis* has a similar range of meaning.

In general usage, for instance, a charming woman is literally a "woman of grace" (Prov. 11:16). A prostitute can be described as "gracefully alluring" (Nah. 3:4). The term can express the idea of receiving "approval" or "favor," as with Mary and Jesus finding favor in the eyes of others (Luke 1:30; 2:52). Usually favor was something sought by inferiors of superiors and, conversely, something granted by a superior to an inferior. The Greek term could be used as well to express thanksgiving for a favor received (Luke 17:9). Such general uses of the language find ample parallels in the nonbiblical literature of the time, with even such phrases as "grace to you and peace" occurring, a phrase assumed by many to be uniquely biblical.

There is in the Bible, however, a distinct use of the language of

78

grace with reference to God. God alone is regularly described as being gracious and capable of offering grace and mercy to humans. Humans can never offer grace to God. It is this special use of the terminology that will be explored in this chapter.

Graciousness as a Divine Attribute

The Bible rarely describes God in terms of particular attributes. Later nonbiblical creedal statements may speak of God as infinite, immortal, and so forth, but in the Bible the emphasis is much more on how God relates to humankind and the divine expectations of the creature. But there is a set of terms that occurs in a number of different contexts that does seem to describe divine attributes, and one of these is *hannun*, "gracious." This term is used almost exclusively of God. When at Moses' request God reveals the essentials of the divine character, the first two words that are used are *rahum* and *hannun*, "merciful" and "gracious" (Exod. 34:6; cf. Joel 2:13; Jonah 4:2; Pss. 86:15; 103:8; 111:4; 116:5; 145:8; Neh. 9:17, 31; 2 Chron. 30:9). The order of these two terms is at times reversed, but they are used together to emphasize the essential benevolence of God toward humanity.

God can and does intervene on occasion to deliver people from grave threats and provide for them (Ps. 86:15; 111:4–9; 116:4–8). God can and does show favor or act graciously to humankind (Jonah 4:1–11; cf. Ps. 145:8–9). God is *rahum* and *hannun*, merciful and gracious, graciously showing mercy and mercifully acting graciously. This characteristic, though not simply automatic, behavior on the part of God provides the basis of hope for Israel and for countless individuals across the centuries.

In fact, Israel's whole history can be described as a story of divine grace. Sometimes the explicit language is present and sometimes it is not, but the story recounts God's gracious care and guidance of Israel, including even the divine judgment that is at times experienced by Israel. From the covenants made with Noah and Abraham, to the deliverance of the people of Israel from Egypt, the covenant at Sinai, and the coming of God's glory to be with the people, God's grace was the driving power. Through the period of the monarchy with the covenant made with David, to the rise of prophets to provide guidance and correction, down to the rescue of Israel once again, this time from the exile in Babylon, God's grace was extended. In light of this amazing and gracious story, it is not surprising that in the New Testament the grace of God, especially for Paul, becomes a dominant theme.

Seeking Divine Favor

The grace of God was often sought. There was no way to earn it, of course, but the belief that God was essentially gracious and merciful prompted many to call out for God's favor. This divine graciousness was sometimes extended to individuals who were not actively seeking it. Noah was shown divine favor quite unexpectedly, and thereby was delivered, with his family and representatives of all living kind, from the great flood (Gen. 6:8). God made Joseph "favorable," or attractive, in the eyes of the overseer of the prison (Gen. 39:21). Those who are loyal and faithful often find favor in "the sight of God and of people" (Prov. 3:4). Likewise, those who "walk uprightly" may well receive divine favor (Ps. 84:11). God also shows favor to the humble (Prov. 3:34). And the poor and needy, especially, may call expectantly to God to be gracious to them (Ps. 86:1, 16; cf. Exod. 22:27). But there was no way to compel God's favor; one could only appeal to divine grace (Dan. 9:18).

There are a number of entreaties for divine grace by individuals preserved in the Psalms. "Be gracious to me, O LORD, for I am languishing" are words addressed to God from one seeking healing (Ps. 6:2; cf. 30:8–10; 31:9) and are accompanied by a report that the prayer was heard (6:9; cf. 30:1–3, 11–12; 31:21–22). Psalm 25 records a cry for help from one who is stricken with guilt and under attack (25:11, 16–19; cf. 41:4; 51:3ff.). Sometimes the supplicant may be a person of integrity who is being oppressed in some manner by the wicked; "redeem me, and be gracious to me" is the prayer (26:11; cf. 140:1–13). The Hebrew terms translated "be gracious" and "supplication" (which comes from the same basic word for grace) occur in numerous passages in the Psalms (4:1; 6:2, 9; 25:16; 26:11; 27:7; 28:2, 6; 30:10; 31:9, 22; 41:4, 10; 51:1; 55:1; 56:1; 57:1; 86:3, 16; 116:1; 119:29, 58, 132, 170; 130:2; 140:6; 143:1), attesting how often the God known to be "merciful and gracious" was sought in hope and confidence that favor would be shown.

But with regard to the community of Israel and its need to seek divine favor another dynamic was at work, namely, the ongoing tension between loyalty and apostasy. The importance of God's grace in the life of Israel is laid out in the long prayer Solomon raised to God at the dedication of the temple in Jerusalem, according to the Deuteronomistic theologian. The connection of this prayer with divine grace is somewhat obscured in English (at least in the NRSV) because the term "plea" is used as a translation for the Hebrew designations for the prayers for divine grace. In Hebrew the word "plea" is clearly related to the word "seeking favor" or "grace," both in the verbal and nominal senses.

In 1 Kings 8, Solomon raised his impassioned "plea" before God, seeking God's favor on behalf of his people (8:54, 59). Several circumstances are envisioned (all of which in hindsight surely occurred) where God's people would seek God's favor, where they would plead before God for a favorable outcome from some difficult situation (1 Kgs. 8:28, 30, 33, 38, 45, 47, 49, 52, 54, 59). In all but one instance (8:44–45, a plea for victory), the people are envisioned crying out, pleading, for divine favor when they are facing great difficulty (after defeat, 8:33; in the midst of famine or plague, 8:37–38; or when in the midst of exile they recognize their sinfulness before God, 8:47, 49; cf. Dan. 9:4–19).

From the vantage point of the compilers of the First Testament, were it not for the gracious mercy of God, Israel would not have survived as a people. Their apostasy was simply too great. The prophet Amos recognized that a portion of God's people might survive the destruction the prophet saw coming, but only if "the LORD, the God of hosts, will be gracious to the remnant of Joseph" (Amos 5:15). But if the people show no sign of discernment or contrition, God will not have compassion (Isa. 27:11).

True repentance was the only hope for a wayward people, and Joel thus urged Israel to "return to me [God] with all your heart, with fasting, with weeping, and with mourning; rend your hearts and not your clothing. Return to the LORD, your God, for he is gracious and merciful, slow to anger, and abounding in steadfast love, and relents from punishing" (Joel 2:12–13; cf. Isa. 30:19; Jer. 31:9). The Chronicler reported that King Hezekiah made a similar appeal in his efforts to bring the people who remained in the north after the Assyrian onslaught of 721 BCE together with people in the south. If the people would repent, Hezekiah said, then the gracious mercy of God would surely be extended to them because that was the way God was—*hannun* and *rahum*, gracious and merciful (2 Chron. 30:9).

Grace in the New Testament

The Greek word *charis* (often translated "grace" in the New Testament) was used commonly at the time of Jesus to describe something "pleasant" or "attractive" or to refer to a "kindly attitude" or a "favor" extended. These meanings of "grace" are certainly found in the Second Testament. There is in fact nothing unusual about the use of the term in Luke (it does not appear in Matthew or Mark). Jesus was described as increasing "in wisdom and in years, and in divine and human favor" (Luke 2:52; cf. 2:40). Similarly, Luke wrote, "All spoke well of him [Jesus] and were amazed at the gracious words that came from his mouth," apparently commenting on the pleasant and effective manner of speech Jesus had developed (4:22). In the common greetings that are found in many of the epistles (e.g., Rom. 1:7; 1 Cor. 1:3) the term *charis* is paralleled by the same usage in secular literature. Likewise, the phrase "thanks be to God" (literally, "grace to God"), used commonly in Greek culture, is found several times in the New Testament (e.g., 2 Cor. 8:9).

In the Gospel of John there are four occurrences of *charis*, all within a few short verses in the Prologue (1:14–17). John uses the phrase "grace and truth" twice (1:14, 17) and "grace upon grace" once (1:16). The phrase "grace and truth" may be an example of a literary device called *hendiadys*, where the two nouns are joined with "and" to express something like "genuine graciousness" or "dependable grace." "Grace upon grace" expresses the inexhaustible character of God's gift to the community in Jesus, the incarnate Word. John does not develop the notion of grace, but his work certainly echoes much that the apostle Paul had to say about the character of divine commitment as demonstrated in Jesus Christ.

Of the roughly 150 occurrences of the term *charis* in the New Testament, some 100 of them are found in the letters of Paul. While, as already noted, Paul did use the term *charis* in ways common in his social setting, he also developed his own very special theological use of the term. First of all, while Paul spoke of the "grace of Jesus Christ" (Rom. 16:20; 2 Cor. 13:13), more regularly he assumed God to be the source of grace (e.g., Rom. 5:15; 15:15; 1 Cor. 1:4; 3:10). Paul understood grace as a gift bestowed upon him by God that enabled him to turn his life in a new direction (1 Cor. 15:10). In whatever situation Paul found himself, God's grace was sufficient (2 Cor. 12:9). Indeed, all the spiritual gifts (e.g., prophecy, service, exhortation, teaching, miracles, healings, tongues) are gracious signs of God's care (Rom. 12:6–8; 1 Cor. 12:28–31) and are to be used for the upbuilding of the community. God's grace and Jesus' grace are essentially one and the same (2 Thess. 1:12; Rom. 5:15), but for Paul God was the primary source, and Jesus was the God-appointed means for the effective transmission of divine grace to humankind.

Paul often concluded his letters with a blessing that extended the "grace of Christ" to his readers (Rom. 16:20; 1 Cor. 16:23; Gal. 6:18; Phil. 4:23; 1 Thess. 5:28; 2 Thess. 3:18). What Paul understood the grace of Christ to mean is perhaps best seen in 2 Corinthians and Philippians. The "generous act," that is the "grace," of the Lord Jesus Christ is demonstrated in "that though he was rich, yet for your sakes he became poor, so that by his poverty you might become rich" (2 Cor. 8:9). In Philippians Christ "did not regard equality with God as something to be exploited, but emptied himself, taking the form of a slave, being born in human likeness. And being found in human form, he humbled himself and became obedient to the point of death— even death on a cross" (Phil. 2:6–8). God's grace is seen in the totally unexpected generosity of coming into the midst of humanity in the person of Jesus, who in turn lived a humble life, fully identifying with humankind, even to experiencing a cruel and undeserved execution. By his poverty, by his self-emptying, by his obedience, Christ extended God's gracious mercy, God's merciful grace, to humanity.

For Paul the greatest barrier between God and humankind was human sin, whether willful disobedience and defiance of God's way or simply human weakness that led to error and erosion of community. For many of Paul's Jewish contemporaries, the remedy for this problem was to carefully and faithfully follow the Mosaic law and thereby be forgiven, "justified," before God. Paul, however, believed that it was impossible for anyone to do that. No human being had the capacity to live so faithfully the commandments that righteousness before God could be obtained. And even if one might achieve some measure of "success" in such an effort, there was no way to wipe away all of the sins of the past. Only the gracious intervention by God in Christ Jesus was able to work justification. This is the substance of Paul's discourse in Romans 3–5.

Two passages sum up Paul's conviction:

> For there is no distinction, since all have sinned and fall short of the glory of God; they are now justified by his grace as a gift, through the redemption that is in Christ Jesus, whom God put forward as a sacrifice of atonement by his blood, effective through faith. (Rom. 3:22–25)

> But God proves his love for us in that while we still were sinners Christ died for us. Much more surely then, now that we have been justified by his blood, will we be saved through him from the wrath of God. For if while we were enemies, we were reconciled to God through the death of his Son,

much more surely, having been reconciled, will we be saved by his life. (Rom. 5:8–10)

"Grace" and "faith" are the two most important terms in Paul's religious vocabulary, and both are God's gifts. Ephesians contains a classic summary of Paul's teaching on the efficacy of divine grace:

> But God, who is rich in mercy, out of the great love with which he loved us even when we were dead through our trespasses, made us alive together in Christ—by grace you have been saved—and raised us up with him and seated us with him in the heavenly places in Christ Jesus, so that in the ages to come he might show the immeasurable riches of his grace in kindness toward us in Christ Jesus. For by grace you have been saved through faith, and this is not your own doing; it is the gift of God—not the result of works, so that no one may boast. (Eph. 2:4–9)

With these words Paul's basic insights are expressed. Sin has alienated humankind from God. Only God can provide justification. Keeping the law is impossible. Works cannot bridge the chasm (Rom. 3:21–31). Only because God is graciously merciful, mercifully gracious, is reconciliation possible. Grace is the free gift of God offered in Christ Jesus, who in turn makes possible the salvation, the justification/reconciliation, of which all are in need.

While Paul believed grace to be a gift, he also recognized that, first of all, grace describes God's attitude. Grace is not a commodity in God's heavenly storehouse to be doled out. Rather, grace describes the way God relates to humankind. God is graciously active in seeking humans, bringing healing and restoration to individuals and communities. Grace "abounds," according to Paul (Rom. 5:15; 2 Cor. 4:15). God's grace, God's graciousness, is immeasurably rich, sufficient for all needs (Eph. 2:7). Faith is the mechanism that makes grace effective in human life.

Whether God's grace can be refused or somehow lost is a matter of debate. Some have insisted that, for Paul, grace was absolutely "irresistible" because he believed that God alone determined who was to receive the divine gift and that such a gift could not be refused (Rom. 11:5–6). But Paul did warn the Galatians against those who might claim the power of the law and thereby "nullify the grace of God" (Gal. 2:21). Such folk were in danger of falling "away from grace" (Gal. 5:4). Likewise, Paul warned the Corinthians "not to accept the grace of God in vain" (2 Cor. 6:1), thereby implying that such was indeed a possibility.

For Paul, God's gracious relationship worked reconciliation and created new possibilities for human beings. In the letter to the Galatians Paul celebrated the new community made possible by God's grace through Jesus Christ. The new relationship with God brings with it the "fruit of the Spirit" which "is love, joy, peace, patience, kindness, generosity, faithfulness, gentleness, and self-control. There is no law against such things" (Gal. 5:22–23). That is the best summary of the power of God to refashion humanity into a community of grace, reflecting God's own graciousness.

Some Concluding Reflections

In reflecting upon God's grace it is important to recognize both the relational aspect and the transformative aspect. First and foremost, the story of God's relationship with the world preserved in the Bible is an account of divine graciousness. The most frequent descriptive phrases used in the First and Second Testaments emphasize the grace of God. Repeatedly in the Old Testament God is praised as "gracious and merciful." Appeal is made to God in the confidence that God is graciously predisposed to respond. Forgiveness and restoration is possible because of God's merciful graciousness.

Israel's history and that of the church testifies to the ongoing power of divine grace. Creation was an act of grace. Deliverance and promised hope were the experiences of those who preceded Israel. Election and rescue from Egypt were acts of grace mediated by Moses. And then the covenant and life-directing law were fashioned at Sinai. For nearly a thousand years before the coming of Jesus, God's people were guided, chastised, forgiven, renewed, and rescued again and again because God was "gracious and merciful." After the destruction of Solomon's temple and Jerusalem by the Babylonian armies in 587 BCE, God's people continued by the grace of God and looked for a time when divine grace would bring the renewal and transformation of the world.

The story continued in the New Testament with the announcement of the birth of a child who would manifest the grace of God in a very particular and remarkable manner. God's grace, the New Testament writers proclaimed, was in fact incarnate in Jesus of Nazareth. In the course of Jesus' life—including his death and resurrection—God's graciousness was again revealed. As a consequence of the grace of God in Jesus, the church was created and was given a ministry of proclaiming God's reconciling love, God's redeeming grace.

The apostle Paul, especially, refined the understanding of divine grace as revealed in Christ Jesus, and emphasized the transformative character of divine grace as well as the relational. Just as in the Old Testament, "grace" was first of all the best word to describe the loving, forgiving constancy of God's relationship with humankind. God was indeed mercifully gracious and graciously merciful. Paul experienced that grace in his own life and saw its effects in the new community that arose in response to Jesus.

But the special emphasis that Paul articulated was that it was by grace that justification was made possible, and by justification, transformation. At one time Paul thought that obedience to the Mosaic law was the God-given avenue to divine forgiveness and reconciliation. After he was claimed by God through Christ, however, Paul became certain that only the gracious act by God in Christ Jesus made the needed justification, the declaration of pardon from all sin, possible. Not only did God's grace in Jesus Christ reclaim the individual, it also made possible the creation of a new community, a people who reflected God's graciousness in their interaction with one another and with others in their world. For Paul, and for the biblical account, divine grace is the key to understanding and participating in life as God intends it.

Questions for Discussion

1. How are grace and mercy related to one another in the biblical story and in your experience of divine love?
2. Where and how does divine grace appear and guide the story of the formation and continuation of Israel and the church?
3. What are some of the similarities and differences in the way grace is described in the Old and New Testaments?
4. How and why does Paul connect God's grace with forgiveness, justification, faith, and salvation?

Chapter Nine

Salvation

S alvation is something most people want, many people think they deserve, and some testify to having experienced. "God is salvation," or "Salvation is God's," or simply "salvation" are used in Hebrew personal names recognized in English as Elisha, Isaiah, Hosea, and Joshua, to name but a few. And of course, there is Jesus, a name that comes through the Latin transliteration of the Greek rendering of the Hebrew *jeshuah* (a late form of Joshua), meaning "salvation." Early on Matthew interpreted the name with "for he [God or Jesus?] will save his people from their sins" (Matt. 1:21). Many people assume that "Jesus saves" is a legitimate summary of the biblical message, though that phrase is nowhere to be found in the Bible.

A large complex of terms is often found in association with the Hebrew and Greek terms for "salvation" that includes words that mean "watch over," "defend," "support," "heal," "raise up," "pull out," "remember," and "answer." These terms give some sense of the impact that "salvation" had, but each of them has its own nuance that does not directly explicate "salvation." These terms will not be examined here. Even words such as "redeem," "ransom," "judge," and "righteousness" that are more closely connected to "salvation" will only be considered where there seems to be a direct connection.

Probably the most important insight that a close examination of the Bible offers on this theme is that "salvation" generally indicates receiving help of some sort to deal with a crisis. Although "salvation" is frequently assumed to mean being rescued from a difficulty, more times than not in the Bible, "salvation" means being enabled to deal with some grave difficulty. With this in mind, let us explore the theme in some detail.

The Language of Salvation

The Old Testament has a number of terms derived from one basic root, *ysh'*. The primary verb is *hoshia'*, meaning "to render help in some fashion." Its nominal form can be rendered "savior" (Judg. 3:9, 15; Isa. 19:20; 43:11). This verb is at times found in contexts where legal terms such as *ga'al* (redeem), *padah* (ransom), *shapat* (judge), and *sedeq* (righteousness) are found. There are also several nouns based on the verb that convey much the same meaning with only slight differences in nuance that must be determined from particular contexts. These are translated variously as "salvation," "deliverance," "rescue," "help," and "victory." Most of the references are to immediate assistance in the face of "this world" threats.

In the New Testament the primary verb is *sozo*, with the noun *soteria* meaning "salvation." The English term "salvation" is derived from the Latin used to translate the Greek. In the Gospels, exorcism of demons and healing from disease is often described with the language of salvation. Sometimes rescue from physical peril or death is the issue. But there also is introduced a more "religious" understanding of "salvation," a more "other world" and "beyond this life" emphasis, that spoke to people living in a culture where mystery religions offered a variety of "saviors" from the trials of earthly existence.

In many dictionaries of the Bible the meaning of the language of salvation has often been related to an Arabic root meaning "to be spacious" or "to enlarge," the idea being that deliverance or salvation was from circumstances that were confining or constricting, that needed expanding and enlarging. More recent research suggests a different background, however, identifying a proto-Semitic root meaning "to bring help" or "assistance." While there are texts in which the idea of a need for liberation from restricting circumstances is expressed, that situation is generally addressed using different Hebrew verbs (Pss. 4:1; 18:16–19; 25:17; 31:8; 118:5).

Salvation at the Reed Sea

Foundational to the biblical understanding of salvation is Israel's experience of delivery from bondage in Egypt, the escape at the Reed Sea (*yam suph*, "Sea of Reeds"). The account of this "salvation" or "deliverance" (the same Hebrew word is translated with two different English words) is found in the prose narrative in Exodus 14 and in a poetic song of victory in Exodus 15. The narrative pictures Moses trying to calm the people fleeing from Egypt when they saw that Pharaoh's army was in hot pursuit (Exod. 14:9–12). Moses said, "Do not be afraid, stand firm, and see the deliverance [*yeshu'ah*] that the LORD will accomplish for you today; for the Egyptians whom you see today you shall never see again" (14:13).

There follows a description of God's bringing assistance to Israel in the form of an "angel" and a "pillar of cloud" (14:19; cf. 14:24), a "strong east wind" (14:21), and the movement of the waters (14:21–29). From the narrator's point of view, it was clear that the Lord had fought for Israel and had overcome the Egyptian army (14:18, 25, 27, 31). The conclusion was drawn that "the LORD saved [*yosha'*] Israel that day from the Egyptians" (14:30). By coming to Israel's assistance in the midst of grave danger, God did a "great work" (14:31) and prompted Israel to sing in testimony, "The LORD is my strength and my might, and he has become my salvation [*yeshu'ah*]" (15:2).

The subtle but important nuance of the terms *yasha'* (save) and *yeshu'ah* (salvation) can be recognized when compared with the language used in Exodus 3:7–10, 6:6–8. Moses is sent to announce to the people that God has heard their cry and will "come down to deliver [from the verb *natsal*, "to snatch away"] them from the Egyptians, and to bring them up [from the verb *'alah*, "to go up"] out of that land" (3:8). Later Moses is instructed to say, "I am the LORD, and I will free you [*yatsa'*, "bring you out"] from the burdens of the Egyptians and deliver [*natsal*] you from slavery to them. I will redeem [*ga'al*] you with an outstretched arm and with mighty acts of judgment" (6:6). In these verses God's intervention at the exodus is described in the language of removing Israel from difficulty. In the description of "salvation" as experienced (Exod. 14–15), the emphasis is on how God brought relief into the situation—salvation *in* not *from*.

This same use of the basic language for salvation (*hoshia'*, *yeshu'a*, *yesha'*, *mosha'ot*, and *teshu'a*) is found in a number of accounts relating various victories ("salvations") on the part of Israel. Gideon prayed for and received a sign that God would deliver/save his people (Judg. 6:37–38). God then reiterated the divine pledge by assuring Gideon, "I will deliver you" (7:7). David was given "a great victory" (literally, "a great salvation") over the Philistine Goliath (1 Sam. 19:5), and as God's agent David was empowered to save Israel from the Philistines (2 Sam. 3:18). Similar references are made to victories/salvations associated with kings Jeroboam (2 Kgs. 14:27), Jehoshaphat (2 Chron. 20:17), and Hezekiah (2 Chron. 32:22). All of this language recalls God's "salvation" experienced at the time of Israel's exodus from Egypt and emphasizes again that salvation/victory occurs in the midst of difficult situations, not removal from them.

God, the Savior

The Bible strongly affirms that there is but one Savior, though there may be "saviors" who act under divine authorization. Isaiah, particularly, emphasized the singularity of God as Savior: "For I am the LORD your God, the Holy One of Israel, your Savior" (Isa. 43:3; cf. 45:15; Jer. 14:8). And again: "I, I am the LORD, and besides me there is no savior. I declared and saved and proclaimed, when there was no strange god among you; and you are my witnesses, says the LORD" (Isa. 43:11–12; cf. 45:21; Hos. 13:4). No other god, idol, king, or power can "save" (Isa. 26:18; 45:20; 46:7; 47:13; Hos. 13:10; 14:3; Jer. 11:12). There were numerous times when Israel, collectively as a nation, sought and/or received God's "salvation." During the Assyrian invasion in 701 BCE (Isa. 37:20) and the Babylonian attack in 588 BCE (Jer. 42:11), God's deliverance was sought. And in the midst of exile (Jer. 30:10–11; 31:7; 46:27), Israel longed for salvation. Occasions of sin (Isa. 64:5), ritual impurity (Ezek. 36:29; 37:23), and sickness (Jer. 8:20–21) also prompted calls for deliverance/salvation. God's intervention brings something to those in distress and strengthens them. Salvation is like the fortifications of a city under siege (Isa. 26:1; 60:18), like water for the thirsty (Isa. 12:3). God's people are not removed from hard times but enabled to overcome them.

This same emphasis continues in the New Testament with one extremely important qualification. God is clearly the Savior who acts on behalf of Israel, and on behalf of Gentiles as well (Luke 1:47; Rom. 5:9–10; 8:24; 9:27; 11:14, 26; 1 Cor. 1:18–21; Eph. 2:4–8; 1 Tim. 1:1; 2:3–6; 4:10; 2 Tim. 1:9; Titus 2:11; Rev. 7:10; 19:1). That is unquestioned. But God's salvation and acts as Savior in the New Testament are also often related to Jesus Christ. Jesus too is called "savior" (Luke 2:11; John 4:42; Acts 13:23; Phil. 3:20; Titus 1:3–4; 2 Pet. 1:11; 2:20; 3:2, 18). Acts declares, "There is salvation in no one else" (Acts 4:12). God remains the source of salvation, but Jesus is hailed as the mediator of God's loving action. The close identification of Jesus with God (e.g., John 1:1–18; 20:28; Heb. 1:8; Titus 2:13) implied, if it did not unambiguously assert, that Jesus was divine and therefore rightly exercised the role of Savior.

There were always "false gods" that contended with God as "saviors." Both in the times before Jesus and during the early centuries of the Christian movement, polytheism and idol worship presented a challenge. The prophets lambasted Israel for the absurdity of trusting in human-made idols. Isaiah and Jeremiah, especially, lampooned idol worship with biting satire (Isa.

44:9–20; Jer. 10:1–10). For the average Israelite, the allure of the fertility religion Baalism continued for a very long time, as archaeological artifacts—idols, altars, fertility ornaments—testify.

In New Testament times the threat of polytheism continued, but there was added to it at least two twists. First, versions of Hellenistic religion known as mystery religions were built around the myth of a supernatural savior that came to earth to save humankind. This savior brought peace into the lives of the faithful. The allure was especially strong, for the "mysteries" were aimed at individuals and did not require collective, family, or national agreement.

Second, the imperial cult of Rome became stronger in the century before and during the earthly life of Jesus. Some of the Hellenistic kings had earlier been considered as "divine saviors" (e.g., Alexander the Great and Ptolemy I). This custom was adopted by Rome. Beginning with Julius Caesar, the Roman Senate declared a number of emperors divine. In the beginning, this was done posthumously, but then later, with the emperors Caligula, Nero, Domitian, Commodus, and Diocletian, the claim was made while the emperor still lived. Worship of the divine emperor was expected, with titles such as "god," "lord and god," and "savior" ascribed. Compliance with the demand to worship a human being as though he were "lord and god" was impossible for Jews and Christians and resulted in their persecution in certain places and times. Over against the threats of polytheism and the imperial cult, the biblical witness continued firm that God alone was the only living Savior.

Part of the "success" of the biblical testimony rested on the affirmation that God was faithful and to be trusted. This, of course, is basic to the story of God's relationship with Israel and the church. The trustworthiness of God as Savior is further underscored by the association of salvation language with several terms that are drawn from the sphere of law. In Isaiah 43, for instance, Israel's Savior, God, has "redeemed" (*ga'al*) and "ransomed" (*padah*) Israel (43:2–3). "Redeem" (*ga'al*) is particularly noteworthy. To redeem was a legally binding obligation aimed at protecting one's kin or buying back one's freedom if it were lost. God, in acting as Israel's Redeemer (Isa. 41:14; 44:6; 49:7, 26; 60:16; 63:5, 8, 9), assumed this legal responsibility. God is Israel's Savior (Isa. 63:8), bound by oath and an everlasting covenant (Isa. 45:22–23; 61:8–10) that is maintained by God's steadfast love and faithfulness (Isa. 33:6; 63:7). "Ransom" (*padah*), not as widely used, is found particularly in Deuteronomy and a few other places (e.g., Exod. 6:6; 15:13; Isa. 41:14; 44:21–28) in reference to God's action releasing Israel from Egyptian bondage (Deut. 7:8; 9:26; 13:6; 15:15; 21:8; 24:18; 2 Sam. 7:23). As with "redeem," "ransom" has a specific legal/ritual background (Exod. 13:13–15; 21:8, 30; Num. 3:45–51; 18:15–16; 35:12, 19). "Ransom," like "redeem," has legal overtones that emphasize the reliability of God. The Savior is trustworthy.

Seeking Salvation

In the Bible there are numerous appeals to the divine Savior for help. In nearly half of the psalms, for instance, there are one or more occurrences of some form of salvation language. There are a number of psalmlike passages elsewhere in the Bible where this language also occurs (Gen. 49:2–27; Deut. 32:15–18; 33:26–29; 1 Sam. 2:1–10; 2 Sam. 22:3–51 [cf. Ps. 18]; 23:2–7; 1 Chron. 16:8–36 [cf. Ps. 96:1–13; 105:1–15; 106:1, 47]; 2 Chron. 6:41–42 [cf. Ps. 132:8–10]; Isa. 38:10–20; Lam. 3–4; Jonah 2:2–9; Hab. 3:2–19; Luke 1:68–79; 2:29–32). "Save me" is a much repeated plea (e.g., Pss. 3:7; 6:4; 7:1; 22:21; 54:1).

Collectively and individually, people in the Bible called on God for salvation in a variety of settings. Sometimes Israel's leaders were directed by God to "save" the people (Judg. 6:14–15; 2 Sam. 3:18; 2 Kgs. 14:27). But more often God was appealed to directly for deliverance: from military enemies (1 Sam. 14:23), from personal enemies (Pss. 3:6; 7:1; 109:31), from illness (Pss. 6:4; 31:2, 16; Isa. 38:20), from disaster and death (Ps. 68:19–20; Matt. 8:25).

A number of images were developed to express the abundance of the salvation offered and effected by God. Salvation/victory was set around the people as "walls and bulwarks" (Isa. 26:1; cf. 60:18). God wears the "helmet of salvation" (Isa. 59:17; cf. Eph. 6:17). God was the Rock of salvation (Deut. 32:15; Pss. 62:2; 89:26). Isaiah contributed the "wells of salvation" (Isa. 12:3). Divine salvation shines forth "like a burning torch" (Isa. 62:1; cf. 49:6; Matt. 5:14). The "horn of salvation" is praised (Ps. 18:2; Luke 1:69). These are all metaphors drawing on the deep significance of salvation.

In the First Testament there is little connection of "salvation" with "sin." In Psalm 51, the psalmist, after pleading with God for forgiveness from numerous sins and transgressions, does ask God, "Restore to me the joy of your salvation, and sustain in me a willing spirit" (51:12). But this is the exception, not the rule. Another set of Hebrew terms is used when speaking of the forgiveness of sin: *kaphar* (cover); *salach* (send away); *natsa* (lift up or away). Thus, the term "salvation" is not directly equated with forgiveness and mercy. Nonetheless, it certainly is understood as the condition that follows from such divine action.

In the Second Testament, on the other hand, forgiveness from sin becomes a major emphasis, though the specific language of salvation is used sparingly. "Christ Jesus came into the world," Paul wrote, "to save sinners" (1 Tim. 1:15; cf. Matt. 1:21; John 3:17). The manifestation of salvation was primarily in Jesus' healings/exorcisms and acts of forgiveness (e.g., Matt. 9:1–6; Mark 2:5–10; Luke 5:20–24). In Greek the word for "save" can also be translated "make well" (thus Mark 5:34; 10:52). Thus, from Luke's point of view, when healing, Jesus could just as easily pronounce the forgiveness of sin and declare the saving effect of faith (Luke 7:46–50). Christ's death and resurrection were understood as the guarantee of divine forgiveness of sin (e.g., Acts 2:38; 3:19; 10:43; 1 Cor. 15:3) and were connected with divine salvation (Rom. 1:3–4, 16; Heb. 5:9; 1 Pet. 1:3–10).

Salvation and Eschatology

In the first instance, salvation is what God brings into a situation to assist in overcoming a crisis. In both the Old and New Testaments, salvation is experienced by believers in the here and now. Moses knew God's salvation/deliverance at the Reed Sea (Exod. 14:13; 15:2). Hannah sang in praise of divine salvation/victory after she dedicated her son Samuel to the Lord (1 Sam. 2:1). In Psalm 18 the king celebrated the "new reality" that salvation brought. The psalm begins with praise: "I love you, O LORD, my strength. The LORD is my rock, my fortress, and my deliverer, my God, my rock in whom I take refuge, my shield, and the horn of my salvation, my stronghold. I call upon the LORD, who is worthy to be praised, so I shall be saved from my enemies" (Ps. 18:1–3). A description of the grave difficulties faced by the king (18:4–6) is followed by a description of divine deliverance (18:7–19). The king and his people felt confirmed (18:20–30). The "shield of your [God's] salvation" (18:35) assured the defeat of the king's enemies and ended aggression (18:31–50). God's salvation was worked in the real world with real consequences.

When Jesus entered the home of Zacchaeus, he announced, "Today salvation has come to this house" (Luke 19:9). What were the confirming phenomena? Zacchaeus pledged to give half of all he had to the poor and to restore fourfold any he had defrauded (19:8). A tax collector, a sinner, was transformed (19:2, 7). On another occasion a woman with a gravely ill daughter came to Jesus and begged him to come to her house, convinced that if Jesus would lay his hands on the child, she would be made well (Mark 5:23). Jesus did, and the child, who had died by the time Jesus arrived, was restored (5:35–42). The salvation of God had immediate consequences.

But salvation also has a "not yet" aspect. The exilic Isaiah looked for a time to come when God's servant would be "a light to the nations, that my [God's] salvation may reach to the end of the earth" (Isa. 49:6; cf. 52:7–10; 62:1). "On a day of salvation" God preserved the servant and pledged the servant as a "covenant to the people" (49:8). Incredible changes in the physical world and in society will take place (49:9–13). Heaven and earth will pass away, but God's salvation will last forever (51:6–8). But there is yet a time of waiting, a time before God's salvation is fully realized, and in that "in-between time" the requirement to pursue justice is the guide (56:1; 59:9–20).

Paul emphasized the same eschatological character of salvation. It has come, but it is not yet complete. There is still a day of reckoning ahead when God's judgment will come. Those who believe will be secured in divine salvation (1 Cor. 1:21; 10:33; 15:2; Rom. 5:9–10; 8:22–25; 10:11–13). Jesus has come, but the return of the Savior is yet awaited, who will "transform the body of our humiliation that it may be conformed to the body of his glory, by the power that also enables him to make all things subject to himself" (Phil. 3:21). Salvation is here and now but yet to be complete.

Some Concluding Reflections

The biblical understanding of salvation is rooted in historical reality. First and foremost, the language of salvation was used with reference to actual deliverances from oppressive powers and victories over enemies. Divine salvation was able to remove the obstacles of political as well as physical threats. But God did not "pluck" people out of hard situations and place them in some non-historical sphere. Rather, God brought the necessary resources, divine and human, to meet the situation and overcome it in "real" time. Israel's deliverance from Egypt became a paradigm for what salvation involved.

God alone is Savior. When Jesus was called Savior in the New Testament, a very bold claim was advanced. Eventually the doctrine of the Trinity would be developed to try to explain the unexplainable—how a human being can also be divine. The insistence on the singularity of God as Savior was made in a world where many gods were worshiped and invoked to save. In New Testament times, the mystery religions and the imperial cult advanced claims of "saviors." But the Bible insists that there is but one Savior, namely, the God of Israel, the God and Father of Jesus Christ.

Since God's people have experienced in times past the salvation of God, it is understandable and appropriate for them to call upon God for deliverance. Circumstances of threat like war, famine, and oppression supplied numerous occasions when the people called out for salvation. Later, when in Greek the term "to save" also could be translated "to heal," deliverance from sickness and demon possession became occasions for salvation as well. At numerous points across history God's salvation was experienced, but there was always a future, more to come, the complete salvation and restoration of the creation. To hope for salvation in the future is justified, but such a hope should not cloud the fact that salvation has already come.

Questions for Discussion

1. How is God's salvation described as helping people in dire circumstances rather than removing them from difficulty? Does that still seem to prevail?
2. How does the exodus story color the way salvation/victory is presented elsewhere in the Bible?
3. What are some of the situations where the Bible suggests a call for salvation is appropriate? How can salvation be something that happens repeatedly and at the same time be something already secured by God?
4. If there are two Saviors, God and Christ, are there two Gods? Why or why not?

Chapter Ten

People of God

The idea that Israel and/or the church is, or has been, "the people of God" is common among people of Jewish and Christian faith. While the exact phrase "people of God" or "people of the Lord" is not used often in the Bible, there are frequent references to people (communities and individuals) where God is the referent: my people, your people, his people. Such terms underscore the close connection between God and human beings.

But there have been problems associated with this theme. Some Jews and Christians have used this language and idea in an exclusive manner to set themselves apart from other people. Some biblical passages lead to the assumption that God cares only for Jews or only for Christians, depending upon who the interpreters are. Sometimes Jews are understood as the only people of God, with all other human beings, all Gentiles, standing on the outside of divine love. At other times Christians have claimed that sole relationship with God, denying the inclusion of others, particularly the Jews.

The biblical text is consistent about one matter. It is God who establishes and maintains the relationship with the humans that constitute God's people. The constituents of the group may at times vary in scope, but it is always the divine love that gives the relationship its significance. The concern of this chapter is the identity of the "people who belong to God" rather than the "people who think God belongs to them."

The Biblical Language

There are some fourteen Hebrew and Greek terms that are translated "people" in the Bible. These terms refer to different categories of people, such as crowds, inhabitants of a place, individuals, assemblies of people, and so forth. In this chapter, however, two primary Hebrew terms used in reference to peoples and nations in the Old Testament will be considered, as well as one Greek term.

The first Hebrew term is *goy*. This word is often translated "nation" (e.g., Gen. 10:5, 20, 31, 32; 17:16; 18:18; 22:18; 26:4; Isa. 2:2, 4) and tends to designate territory. Sometimes Israel is the referent (Exod. 19:6; 33:13), especially when the term is used by or in contrast to outsiders and enemies of Israel (Deut. 4:6–8; 26:5; Ps. 83:5). Sometimes the northern kingdom, Israel, and the southern kingdom, Judah, are called "nations" (e.g., Isa. 1:4; 10:6; Jer. 5:9, 29; 7:28; Ezek. 2:3; 37:22), especially when they are charged with being sinful and rebellious (Deut. 32:28; Isa. 1:4; 10:6; Jer. 5:9, 29; 7:28; 9:8; 12:17).

More often, however, *goy* or its plural *goyim* are used with reference to non-Hebrews (e.g., Exod. 9:24; 34:10; Lev. 25:44; Deut. 15:6; 1 Kgs. 5:11). (The term '*ibri*, which is translated "Hebrew," is always used in contexts where non-Hebrews are speaking about Hebrews or being contrasted to them. It is not a term chosen as a self-reference by the people called Israel [e.g., Exod. 1:15–16, 19; 2:7; 3:18; 5:3; 1 Sam. 4:6, 9; 13:3, 19].) In some contexts the term *goy* has a definitely negative nuance as it is applied with reference to idolatrous or hostile peoples (e.g., Lev. 8:24, 28; 1 Kgs. 14:24; 2 Kgs. 17:8, 11, 15, 26, 29; Ezek. 4:13). In postbiblical Hebrew, *goy* and *goyim* came for a time to be used derogatively of non-Jews, but in modern times the terms are used more neutrally with reference to Gentiles.

The second Hebrew word used to refer to people is '*am*. This term tends to emphasize blood relationships. The term can be used of humankind as a whole (Gen. 11:6) and of particular communities such as the inhabitants of a city (Gen. 19:4; Jer. 29:16, 25) or a locality (Jer. 37:12), of retainers and people bearing arms (Gen. 14:16; 32:8; Judg. 3:18; 8:5; 1 Sam. 11:11; 1 Kgs. 20:10), and of people in general (Gen. 50:20; Exod. 33:16; Josh. 5:5; Jer. 36:9). *'Am* can designate foreign (i.e., non-Israelite) people (Exod. 21:8; Deut. 28:32; Ezek. 3:5). The phrase *'am ha'arets* (the people of the land) referred usually to landed male citizens (e.g., 2 Kgs. 11:14, 18–20; 15:5) and came to be used in its plural form (peoples of the land) by some of the returnees from the exile in Babylon to designate those they considered "impure" (Ezra 10:2, 11; Neh. 10:31).

But *'am* was also used with a special nuance. Israel was singled out as God's elected, chosen people. *'Am*, Israel, is called "the Lord's people" (Num. 11:29; 1 Sam. 2:24), "my [God's] people" (Exod. 3:7, 5:1), "holy people" (Deut. 7:6; Isa. 62:12; 63:18), and "a treasured possession" (Exod. 19:5; Deut. 7:6; 14:2; 26:18). Since the term *'am* occurs quite frequently in the Old Testament, each context becomes critical in determining the nuance that is intended.

In the New Testament the terminology is somewhat less complex. While there are a number of terms that are used with reference to nations and groups (e.g., *ethnikos/ethnos* = Gentile; *genos* = race/family; *demos* = people/assembly; *ochlos* = crowd), one particular term, *laos* (people), was used predominantly in reference to Israel. Sometimes the term refers to a crowd or the populace in general (Luke 3:15; Acts 3:12; 4:1; Matt. 27:64) or to the common people in contrast to their leaders (Matt. 26:5; Luke 19:48; 20:6, 19). But more frequently *laos* refers to Israel as God's special people. In references to Old Testament traditions (Matt. 4:16; Mark 7:6; Acts 7:34; 13:17) as well as in identifying the people among whom Jesus lived and worked (e.g., Matt. 1:21; 2:4; Luke 3:18; 6:17), the term for "people" is *laos*. Problems arose, however, when in the course of time, the church, combining both Jews and Gentiles, came to be called by some the "Israel of God" (Gal. 6:16; and especially in postbiblical Christian writings).

God's People as Family

The term *'am*, in its simplest meaning, emphasized kinship, family, clan—particularly paternal relationships (Gen. 19:38; Jer. 37:12; Ruth 1:10–16). Israel's story was told as the account of how one family, descended from Jacob/Israel (Gen. 49:1–28; Exod. 1:1–7), became the special people of God, "my people" (Exod. 3:7), when they were released from bondage in Egypt (Exod. 3:8–10). Theoretically, every person that belonged to "Israel" was related to all others as a member of the family (brothers, sisters, cousins, nephews, nieces, etc.). The tradition, however, indicates that there were many others, "a mixed crowd," with no genetic connection to "Israel" the son of Isaac, who came out of Egypt at the exodus (Exod. 12:38).

The family, the people, became self-aware, in a sense, at Sinai. To be sure, the story is told in retrospect and reaches back to claim Abraham and Sarah as the initiators of the family (Gen. 12–23), but it was after the escape from Egypt that Israel as a people was defined. Leading up to the deliverance at the Reed Sea (the "Red Sea" in the Septuagint), the captives were claimed by God as "my firstborn son" and then repeatedly called "my people" (Exod. 4:22; cf. 3:7; 5:1; 7:16; 8:1, 20; 9:1, 13; 10:3). Language of adoption was used when God said, "I will take ["adopt"; cf. Esth. 2:7; Gen. 48:5–6] you as my people, and I will be your God. You shall know that I am the LORD your God, who has freed you from the burdens of the Egyptians" (Exod. 6:7). Then, as the people were gathered at the base of Mount Sinai, God directed Moses to say, "Thus you shall say to the house of Jacob, and tell the Israelites: You have seen what I did to the Egyptians, and how I bore you on eagles' wings and brought you to myself. Now therefore, if you obey my voice and keep my covenant, you shall be my treasured possession out of all the peoples. Indeed, the whole earth is mine, but you shall be for me a priestly kingdom and a holy nation" (Exod. 19:3–6).

It was by covenant that Israel became God's people, set apart as a "holy nation [*goy*]" for service as a "priestly kingdom" (Exod.

19:6; cf. 33:13; Deut. 4:6). The language of covenant included "father/son" terminology (see chapter 2), and that fit well with the idea of Israel being a family. God was the Father in the same way that God was later Father to David the king by covenantal adoption (Pss. 2:7; 89:26–29; 2 Sam. 7:14). Each of the parties of the covenant had obligations. The "children" (Israel) were to live in accordance with the Ten Commandments and the other ordinances and statutes of God (Exod. 20:1ff.; Deut. 4:40; 5:1–21; 26:17–19; Lev. 26:3–12). The "Father" (God) promised blessing (Deut. 26:15), protection and deliverance (Pss. 3:8; 28:9; 29:11; Hab. 3:13; Joel 3:16). Only out of great love did God choose to deliver Israel from Egypt to become a prized possession (Deut. 7:7–8). In response, Israel was expected to "acknowledge that the LORD is God; there is no other besides him" (Deut. 4:35; cf. 4:39).

The story of God's people in the First Testament is a mixture of success and failure. The Davidic dynasty lasted for over four hundred years in Judah, a long time for any one dynasty. But the prophets told of repeated disobedience and warned of judgment to come. Amos lamented over Israel as one already dead because of the northern nation's transgressions (Amos 5:2–7, 10–13; 8:2–12). Indeed, several decades after Amos, the Assyrians utterly destroyed the northern kingdom. Jeremiah charged Judah in a similar manner (Jer. 2:4–37; 5:1–17). And before his death Jeremiah saw the destruction of Judah and Jerusalem.

Remarkably, however, the prophets hoped for a future that would include the renewal of Israel's relationship with God and an expansion of those included in the "family." Jeremiah was convinced that God would not finally abandon his people, but would instead fashion a "new covenant" that would enable them to continue in a new relationship (Jer. 31:31–34). Ezekiel likewise awaited a renewal of covenantal blessing (Ezek. 36:22–38). Zechariah hoped for the day when other nations would join the family and become part of God's people (Zech. 2:11). And Isaiah boldly proclaimed a day when Assyria and Egypt, Israel's traditional and hated enemies, would be called by God, "Egypt my people, and Assyria the work of my hands" as they joined with "Israel my heritage" (Isa. 19:25) in the worship of the one God.

Continuity within God's People

When one turns to the Second Testament, one discovers a rich continuity with respect to those who constitute the people of God. New Testament writers continued to refer to Israelites and Jews as God's people, *laos*, distinguishing them from the nations, *'ethnos*. Zechariah, the father of John the Baptist, named Israel as God's people who would be saved by Jesus (Luke 1:68, 77; cf. Matt. 1:21). The song of Simeon, as well, preserves the traditional usage when the salvation "prepared in the presence of all peoples [plural of *laos*]" is recognized as "a light for revelation to the Gentiles [plural of *'ethnos*] and for glory to your people [*laos*] Israel" (Luke 2:31–32).

There was no question whether the Judean community continued to be God's people. In response to one of Jesus' miracles, Luke noted, "Fear seized all of them; and they glorified God, saying, 'A great prophet has risen among us!' and 'God has looked favorably on his people!'" (Luke 7:16). Jesus was remembered interpreting Isaiah's words to "this people" and thereby identifying his audience as a part of "this people" since they, like God's people in Isaiah's time, would not hear (Matt. 13:10–17; cf. Isa. 6:9–10; Mark 4:10–12). Peter addressed his people as "You Israelites" and identified them as members of God's covenantal family (Acts 3:12–13, 25). Likewise Stephen understood the Jews to whom he spoke to be God's people in continuity with their ancestors, inheritors of the covenant made with Moses, and thus liable to punishment just as were their forebears (Acts 7:1–53). Paul understood the Jewish people of his day yet to be God's people (Rom. 11:1–2).

It is clear that during the time of Jesus, and in the decades immediately following his death and resurrection, a primary understanding of the term "God's people" included the "Israel" of the Old Testament and the heirs of that people, namely, the Jews.

In Paul's words in reference to his Jewish kindred, "They are Israelites, and to them belong the adoption, the glory, the covenants, the giving of the law, the worship, and the promises; to them belong the patriarchs, and from them, according to the flesh, comes the Messiah, who is over all, God blessed forever. Amen" (Rom. 9:4–5).

Discontinuity within God's People

The people of God, however, cannot be defined only as the Israel of the Old Testament. Neither contemporary Jews nor Christians will allow such an understanding. Within the New Testament is clear evidence of a developing discontinuity that eventually matured into two religions, Judaism and Christianity, whose adherents have each understood themselves as the people of God.

Discontinuity enters the picture when the church begins to understand itself as the people of God apart from or in the place of Israel and the Jews. Christians initially understood themselves as part of Israel, as another subgroup of Jews within the Jewish family, as one of the Jewish "parties" like the Pharisees or the Sadducees. Most of the first followers of Jesus were Jews and continued to participate in synagogue services and other community gatherings (Matt. 4:20–23; 19:27–28; Luke 4:15; 12:11; Acts 2:1–46). When Jesus began his public ministry, according to Luke, he read a text from the prophet Isaiah first directed to God's people centuries earlier. Jesus then applied the text to himself and to those gathered in the synagogue at Nazareth (Luke 4:16–22). In so doing he underscored what most took for granted at that point, namely, that they would all continue to be Jews, though they followed a radical new rabbi named Jesus.

The identification of the church as Israel, God's people, is seen in Paul's Second Letter to the Corinthians, where he instructs the readers concerning "mixed marriages." Several texts, originally addressed to Israel, are claimed by Paul as words directed to the church (2 Cor. 6:2/Isa. 49:8; 6:16/Lev. 26:11–12; and Ezek. 37:27; 6:17/Isa. 52:11 and Septuagint Ezek. 20:34; 6:18/2 Sam. 7:14; and

Isa. 43:6). Then, in summation, Paul wrote, "Since we have these promises," referring to the Old Testament texts, and in so doing equated the church in Corinth with the historic people of God (2 Cor. 7:1; cf. Heb. 1:5–13; 3:7–11; 10:30, where other words addressed to previous people are claimed as references to Jesus and the church).

As ever increasing numbers of Gentiles joined the Christian movement, the identification of the church as the new Israel, the new people of God, became more explicit. In Philippians, Paul described the Christians by contrasting them with Judaizers: "For it is we who are the circumcision, who worship in the Spirit of God and boast in Christ Jesus and have no confidence in the flesh" (Phil. 3:3). In Acts, Peter reported that the Holy Spirit came upon Gentiles just as upon the Jewish followers of Jesus (Acts 10:44–11:18), and then James, citing Amos 9:11–12 positively, concluded, "Simeon has related how God first looked favorably on the Gentiles, to take from among them a people [*laos*] for his name" (Acts 15:14–15).

In 1 Peter a dramatic new claim was made. The Old Testament was unquestionably a word addressed to the church, directly and, more importantly, solely. Words believed once addressed to Israel and the Jews were no longer so considered. The "living stone" was Christ in whom life was to be found (1 Pet. 2:6; cf. Isa. 28:16). That stone had become a stumbling block for the Jews and had been rejected by them (1 Pet. 2:7–8; cf. Ps. 118:22; Isa. 8:14; 1 Cor. 1:22–24). Therefore, language once used to describe God's people Israel was used in affirmation of the creation of and role of the church: "But you are a chosen race, a royal priesthood, a holy nation, God's own people, in order that you may proclaim the mighty acts of him who called you out of darkness into his marvelous light. Once you were not a people, but now you are God's people; once you had not received mercy, but now you have received mercy" (1 Pet. 2:9–10; Exod. 19:6; Isa. 9:2; 43:18–21; Hos. 1:9; 2:23).

The book of Hebrews was even more explicit. Using a number of Old Testament texts as part of an argument for the superiority of Christ over all other previous avenues to the presence of God, the author then quoted at length from Jeremiah's words concerning God's renewal of covenant (Heb. 8:8–12; cf. Jer. 31:31–34). The conclusion was then made: "In speaking of 'a new covenant,' he [presumably Jeremiah] has made the first one obsolete. And what is obsolete and growing old will soon disappear" (Heb. 8:13). Thus, Christ was "the mediator of a new covenant" (9:15) whose blood was the means by which God chose to "purify our [the believers'] conscience from dead works to worship the living God!" (9:14). This teaching explicitly identified the "people of God" with the church in a way that other images had left at least a little ambiguous (cf. the body of Christ, 1 Cor. 12:12, 27; Eph. 4:15–16; the bride of Christ, Eph. 5:22–33; the branches of Christ the vine, John 15:1–11).

The discontinuity in the New Testament among God's people—namely, the displacement by or supersession of the church over Israel and the Jews as God's people—was understood in the centuries that followed as justification for suppression, oppression, and persecution of Jews by Christians. But more recently, several key passages have been reconsidered with remarkable results. Most important is Romans 9–11, the only passage to consider specifically the relations of Christians and Jews at any length. A careful study of Paul's thoughtful reflections on this matter reveals at least three key matters. First, in the midst of his personal anguish over the Jews' failure to recognize God's saving deed in Jesus Christ, Paul nonetheless believed the Jews—though disobedient—still to be God's people (Rom. 9:2–5; 10:18–21; 11:2–6, 25–32), the "rich root of the olive tree" (11:17–18). Second, Paul's audience consisted of Gentile Christians, not Jews, who were concerned over whether they were a legitimate part of God's people. Paul wrote to assure them that they were (9:24–29; 10:6–13; 11:22–24). The issue was not whether Jews were part of God's people. The question was whether Gentile Christians were included. And third, after Paul wrestled with this matter for a long time, he finally concluded that the whole issue remained a mystery, locked in the inscrutable ways and unsearchable judgments of God (11:33–36).

Paul thus seems to have concluded that though he did not understand exactly how or why, since the coming of Jesus Christ there were now two peoples who belonged to God. Or perhaps better, God's people now had two distinct but eternally related "families" within "the family." Another contribution to the puzzle is found in the conviction that at the end time when God's "new Jerusalem" is established, all peoples, all mortals, will be blessed by God's dwelling with them and will all become God's people (Rev. 21:1–4). In Christ, God's family has already been expanded and opened to believing Gentiles, but in the end, all mortals will know the richness of the divine presence.

Some Concluding Reflections

In the Bible, while there are many terms that can be translated as "people," there are only a few that specifically refer to God's people in a special way. Both in Hebrew and in Greek, these terms stress the "family" character of God's people, as "blood relations," so to speak. From a twelve-tribe family to an olive tree with many branches, the people of God are pictured as interrelated and responsible one to another.

The First Testament describes the history of God's people from its outset from bondage in Egypt to the occupation of the land by the Greeks. There are great successes, such as David's four-hundred-year-long dynasty. But there was ongoing disobedience to God's way, chronicled by the prophets and understood to have been the cause of the destruction first of Israel, the northern kingdom (722 BCE), and then Judah, the southern kingdom (587 BCE). Through all of this history, however, and down until the coming of Jesus, there was always some group of people identified as God's people. They were called Israelites, Judeans, and finally Jews (though this last term is not actually appropriate until around 100 CE).

The Second Testament describes both the continuation of the understanding of the Jews as God's people as well as the emergence of the discontinuous understanding that the church was also in part, or all alone, the people of God. Old Testament texts are quoted in a manner that shows that many still believed the Jews were God's people. Initially, Christians were but a subset among other Jewish groups, but slowly a separation arose between church and synagogue. Some Old Testament passages were interpreted to refer to the church alone and not to the Jews, thereby establishing a basis for teaching that the church had replaced Israel as God's people and justifying, for some, the mistreatment of Jews for centuries to follow. The only extended treatment of this matter by Paul (Rom. 9–11) wisely leaves the issue in the realm of the mystery of God's providence.

Questions for Discussion

1. How can the nuances of different Hebrew and Greek words be recognized and used in understanding matters concerning the "people of God"?
2. What are some of the privileges and burdens of being God's people, as described in the Old Testament?
3. How does the church share in the responsibilities and blessings of inclusion as part of God's people?
4. Why is it important to consider whether and/or how God intends for both Christians and Jews to constitute the people of God? What is the evidence for inclusion of both groups or of only one?

Chapter Eleven

Worship

E ach theme considered in this volume is significantly related to all the others. This is especially true with the themes to be considered in this chapter and the next. In Hebrew and Greek, some of the terms used for "worship" and "service," though translated differently in English, are identical. Whether a term should be rendered as "worship" or "service" can often only be decided on the basis of literary context.

Nonetheless, for the sake of presentation, the larger theme of worship and service will be divided into two chapters. Chapter 11 will concentrate more on what might be called liturgical/cultic (i.e., external) matters, along with various practices involved in the worship of God, while chapter 12 will deal more with the manner in which devotion/ethical concern/motivation (i.e., internal issues) come together in worshipful service of God. To a large degree, however, this is an artificial separation of closely intertwined matters.

The Bible makes reference to numerous types and places of worship, communal as well as individual. People are described as standing, kneeling, and lying prostrate, sometimes with hands extended upward, sometimes with hands folded. Prayer is quite prevalent, and is often supplemented with grain and animal sacrifice, throughout most of the biblical record. Tabernacles, sanctuaries, temples,

synagogues, churches—even the human heart!—are acknowledged as places where God's people have known, and will know,
the presence of God and receive blessing and guidance.

The Language of Worship

In Hebrew there is a rich vocabulary describing various aspects of
worship. "To do service" *('abad)*, for instance, was to act respon-
sibly in cultic matters, to be devoted and loyal to God—in other
words, to "worship" God (e.g., Exod. 3:12; Deut. 6:13; Jer. 2:20).
In Greek, one of the terms translated "worship" *(latreuo)* emphasized public participation in cultic acts (Luke 2:37; Acts 7:7; 26:7).
The more common meaning of the Hebrew term, however, had
to do with acts of service in secular settings. More about this will
be considered in the next chapter.

There were other words as well that relate to the public and
private worship of God. Two terms particularly, one Hebrew and
the other Greek, describe the posture of worshipers. One of the
primary acts of devotion was to prostrate oneself before God: in
Hebrew, *shachah* (e.g., Gen. 22:5; 24:26; Exod. 4:31); in Greek,
proskuneo (e.g., Matt. 2:2, 8, 11; 4:9–10; 1 Cor. 14:25). Further, in
Hebrew the common word for "fear," *yare'*, was used to express
"awe" or "reverence" before God (Exod. 15:11; Deut. 6:2, 13; Ps.
2:11). Somewhat akin was the Greek term *sebo*, used to describe
acts of "showing piety" (Matt. 15:9; Acts 17:23; 18:13). Other
phrases such as "seek the face of the Lord" and "draw near to
God" expressed the desire and intention to seek help and direction from God with devotion and loving adoration (Pss. 22:26;
34:4; Isa. 55:6; 1 Sam. 14:36).

Sacred Time

The Bible is concerned with the matter of when one should worship God, that is, with sacred time—the moments, the days, and
the seasons when God should be acknowledged and praised.
While the psalmist may declare, "I will bless the LORD at all times;

his praise shall continually be in my mouth" (Ps. 34:1), and Paul may urge the Thessalonians to "pray without ceasing" (1 Thess. 5:17), there actually were structured times for worship intended to remind and support the community and individuals in being attentive to God.

Central to sacred time was the Sabbath, later to be paralleled in the Christian church with the Lord's Day. In the Ten Commandments, the commandment establishing the Sabbath day as a day of rest and remembrance is the longest (Exod. 20:8–11; cf. 23:12; 34:21; Deut. 5:12–15). In Exodus, the Sabbath was to be observed as a day of rest by all members of the family, free and slave, and resident aliens as well, and was justified on the basis that on the seventh day after completing the creation God rested (Exod. 20:10–11; cf. Gen. 2:3). In Deuteronomy, the same admonition is based on God's redemption of Israel from slavery (Deut. 5:14–15).

Initially, Sabbath may have been strictly a "negative" observance, that is, marked by the absence of activity, particularly work. But at least after the return of the exiles from the Babylonian captivity (538 BCE) and down to the time of Jesus, while maintaining the prohibition of labor, Sabbath became marked positively by joyous worship of God in homes and in synagogues (in the Diaspora). Sabbath worship included the reading and discussion of sacred texts (Matt. 4:23; Mark 1:21–22; 6:2; Luke 4:16–21, 31–32; Acts 13:27; 15:21; 17:1–2) and became an identifying feature of Jewish life.

There was a time of transition when Jewish Christians continued to observe the Sabbath. But as greater numbers of Gentiles joined the church, patterns changed. While Sabbath observance was not required in the Pauline churches (Gal. 4:10; Col. 2:16), gatherings on the first day of each week, the day of the Lord's resurrection, began to take place. This practice became common among Christians by the late first century and thereafter. The term "the Lord's day" occurs first in Revelation 1:10 and is widely used in postbiblical writings. This day, like the Sabbath for Jews, was marked by gatherings in which the Scriptures were read and the Lord's Supper was shared (Matt. 28:1; Mark 16:2; Luke 4:13–35; Acts 20:7; 1 Cor. 16:2).

The importance of time as a benchmark for worship was also found in the festival calendar, where days and seasons were set apart. The New Moon was an acknowledged monthly festival day in Israel during which the faithfulness of the Lord was especially celebrated (Num. 28:1–10; 1 Sam. 20:5, 18, 24; 2 Kgs. 4:23; Isa. 1:13–14). There were three pilgrimage feasts: (1) Passover, or Unleavened Bread, celebrating Israel's release from Egyptian bondage (Exod. 12:1–13:16; 23:15; 34:18–20, 25; Lev. 23:4–14; Num. 28:16–25; Deut. 16:1–8); (2) Weeks, a spring harvest festival that in postbiblical times came to be a celebration of the giving of the Torah (Exod. 23:16; 34:22; Lev. 23:15–21; Num. 28:26–31; Deut. 16:9–12); and (3) Booths, or Tabernacles, a fall harvest festival that became combined with the celebration of the New Year and was followed by the Day of Atonement, the only prescribed fast day in Israel's cultic calendar (Exod. 23:16; 34:22; Lev. 16:29–34; 23:26–36, 39–43; Num 29:7, 12–32; Deut. 16:13–16; 2 Sam. 12:16–20). Christians later adapted two of these celebrations for their own purposes: Easter for Passover and Pentecost for Weeks. The celebration of Christmas as part of the church's sacred time was a postbiblical development that was not universally adopted.

Other feasts and festivals were celebrated as well. The most notable were the Feast of Purim (see the book of Esther) and the celebration of Hanukkah (see the apocryphal book of 1 Maccabees). Neither of these was widely observed until postbiblical times, but they illustrate once again the importance of time and history in the structuring of worship.

Sacred Space

Just as time was considered important, so was space, though probably to a lesser degree. From the earliest times, the Bible mentions worship in homes, at various established sanctuaries, and in connection with movable shrines, such as the tent of meeting and the ark of the covenant. Over the roughly thousand years of its existence, the temple of Solomon, constructed in the mid-tenth century BCE and refashioned by Herod at the time of Jesus, was the most prominent space mentioned in the Bible dedicated to divine worship.

As the story of Israel came to be told, the first major shrine was the tabernacle that housed the ark of the covenant, which traveled with and led the people of Israel through the wilderness (Exod. 25–30, 35–40). Certainly there had been worship at Sinai during Israel's encampment there (Exod. 19:16–25; 24:1–11; cf. 32:1–6). There is also a tradition about a "tent of meeting" (Exod. 33:7–11) that was absorbed within the tradition of the tabernacle, suggesting that there was a smaller, movable shrine before the more permanent one. Among scholars, there is debate concerning how much the tabernacle tradition was enhanced by a later "reading back" of the temple traditions.

Whatever is to be made of the various scholarly views, the function of the tradition in its current form is clear. The tabernacle provided a tangible symbol of God's ever moving presence with the people. God's glory filled the shrine, giving clear sign that God was accompanying the people and was prepared to receive their worship (Exod. 40:34–38). The tabernacle was principally the place where specified sacrifices were made and where Moses and Aaron "enquired of the Lord" on behalf of the people.

After the people of Israel entered the land of Canaan, the story reports the existence of a number of shrines or sanctuaries. There were ones at Beersheba (Gen. 21:33; 1 Sam. 8:2; Amos 5:5; 8:14), Bethel (Gen. 28:19; 35:1–7; 1 Kgs. 12:26–33; Amos 7:12–13), Gibeon (2 Sam. 2:12–17; 1 Kgs. 3:4–15), Gilgal (1 Sam. 7:16; 13:8–15; Hos. 4:15; 9:15; 12:11; Amos 4:4; 5:5), Shechem (Josh. 24; 1 Kgs. 12:1), and Shiloh (Josh. 21:1–2; 1 Sam. 1:3, 9, 24), to name but a few. Each village of any size had its own "high place" with its own altar. These shrines give evidence that sacred places were important in the religious understanding of the people.

The temple of Solomon certainly provided the most important sacred space. Built on the site of an ancient Jebusite sanctuary within the city of Jerusalem (2 Sam. 5:6–9), the temple for over one thousand years marked the special place where God was to be worshiped. Built with the help of craftsmen provided by King Hiram of Tyre (1 Kgs. 5:1–18), the architecture and furnishings were thoroughly Canaanite or Phoenician (6:1–38; 7:13–50). The Holy of Holies, the most sacred space within the temple, contained the ark of the covenant (8:1–9). When Solomon dedicated the temple, "the glory of the LORD filled the house of the LORD" (8:11), giving assurance of the divine presence. At the same time, it was made clear that God remained in "thick darkness" (8:12), and according to Deuteronomy, only God's name actually was present "at the place that God will choose," later identified by Solomon as the temple in Jerusalem (Deut. 12:11, 14; 1 Kgs. 8:27–30).

During the Davidic monarchy (1000–587 BCE), the temple in Jerusalem (built around 960 BCE) was essentially a royal chapel. Roughly twenty-five years before its destruction by the Babylonians (in 587 BCE), because of reforms brought about by King Josiah (2 Kgs. 23:1–27), the temple began to be used more widely by the general population rather than just by the king and royal entourage. By the time of Jesus, the temple stood at the very center of the cultic life of the community, providing a place for sacrifice, dedication, prayer, and instruction, as well as a place for dealing with civic matters. One could worship in various places throughout the year, but one was expected to go to the temple at least three times a year during the three pilgrimage festivals (of Passover, Weeks, and Tabernacles).

By the close of the biblical period, worship space was primarily to be found in the homes of individuals and in synagogues and churches. The destruction of Jerusalem and the temple by the Romans in 70 CE brought an end to the sacrificial cult centered there. The gathering of the community moved from the temple to other places that became sacred because of their use. Among the numerous Jewish communities that existed around the Mediterranean basin, the synagogue became ever more important as the center of life, a life that very much included the worship of God.

Many Christian congregations met in the homes of believers (1 Cor. 16:19; Rom. 16:5). For Christians, however, sacred space came more and more to be connected with the believing community itself and located there rather than in physical structures (Eph. 2:20; 1 Cor. 3:16–17; 6:19; 1 Pet. 2:4–6). With the indwelling of God's Spirit within individuals and congregations, a new understanding of sacred space began to emerge (1 Cor. 3:16–17; 6:19–20; 2 Cor. 6:16). Worship could and should take place anywhere, for where "two or three are gathered in my name," the disciples were told, "I [Jesus] am there among them" (Matt. 18:20; 28:20; 1 Cor. 5:3–4).

Sacred Practice

Special times and spaces were clearly important in the structure and pattern of worship in ancient Israel, and among Jews and Christians at the close of the biblical period. Within these times and at these places a wide variety of activities occurred that give insight into how and why the people of God worshiped.

Through most of the thousand years or more that provided the historical setting for the biblical accounts, grain and animal sacrifice was probably the most widely practiced communal worship activity. The "community" might be the family of an individual or a much larger gathering of people in times of war or natural calamity. In the biblical period, sacrifice provided a concrete means of repairing breaches in the relationships of one human with another and between humans and God. When one individual or community sinned against another (e.g., Exod. 20:12–17; Deut. 5:16–21) or against God (e.g., Exod. 20:2–11; Deut. 5:6–15), reconciliation was made possible with the offering of prescribed sacrifices (e.g. Lev. 1–7, 16, 22). As strange as it may seem to "modern" people, sacrifice provided a concrete act by which to show repentance with new intentions. At the same time, it also provided a visible, public instrument for beseeching God to provide desperately needed assistance.

The most common sacrifice was the "burnt offering" (Lev. 1).

This was offered as an act of thanksgiving or as an appeal for forgiveness. The burnt offering was totally consumed by the flames of the altar (except in the case of animal sacrifices in which the hide of the sacrificed animal was given to the priest; Lev. 7:8). Such offerings played a major role in public worship and in rites of cleansing (Lev. 12:6, 8; 14:19, 22; 15:15, 30; Num. 28–29).

Another type of sacrifice was called the "sin offering." This name is misleading, since the offering did not have to do with atoning for sin. Rather, the purpose of the sin offering was to provide a means of cleansing or purification when a person or place had become unintentionally defiled. If there was to be a burnt offering, for instance, this was often preceded by a sin offering to ensure the altar was properly cleansed. The blood of the sacrificed animal was sprinkled at appropriate places as part of the ritual. Many passages describe the how and why for the sin offering (Lev. 4:1–5:13; 9:7–21; 12:6; 14:19, 22; 15:15, 30; 16:3, 5; Num. 6:14, 16; 28:15, 22, 30; 29:5, 11, 16, 19). An extension of the sin offering was the development of the Day of Atonement when, annually, a sacrifice for the cleansing of the people and the sanctuary was made (Lev. 16). This was done totally by divine initiative and made it possible to begin each year with a clean slate, so to speak. Of a different order from the sin offering was the "guilt offering" that was to be made in the event of an act of intentional desecration (Lev. 5:14–6:7).

One sacrifice that was offered, the "peace offering" or the "sacrifice of well-being," included the communal eating of the meat of the sacrificial animal as part of the ritual (Lev. 3:1–17; 7:11–36). There were a number of occasions when a peace offering was appropriate, such as offering thanks for safe passage on a journey, recovery from a grave illness, or release from bondage. A peace offering was also offered to fulfill a vow. Further, the peace offering could simply be a free will offering made for no particular reason other than to honor God. The distinctive feature of the peace offering was that the meat of the sacrificed animal had to be eaten within a set time period and sometimes with accompanying specified items. Peace offerings were not made often. When they were, they provided practically the only occasion when the people of Israel ate meat.

As noted above, the temple was the primary place for sacrifices to be offered, especially after King Josiah's reformation and the removal of the local shrines (2 Kgs. 23:1–25). This continued into the time of Jesus. The prophets often criticized the worship of the people at the temple and elsewhere, but not because they thought sacrifice in itself was wrong. In their eyes, the problem was that those who made the offerings were all too often insincere and hypocritical (Isa. 1:11–17; 29:13–14; Jer. 6:20; 7:1–15; Amos 5:21–24). Until the temple's destruction by the Romans in 70 CE there was a set ritual of daily sacrifices that included several burnt offerings accompanied by appropriate cereal and drink offerings (Lev. 6:8–23; Exod. 29:38–42; 30:7–9; Num. 28:3–6; 2 Kgs. 16:15; Ezek. 46:13–15). This ritual was considered most important and was expanded on festival days.

Accompanying the sacrifices, but also quite apart from them, were a number of other acts of worship. Prayers and songs, for instance, were a frequent part of communal and individual worship. The book of Psalms has preserved numerous prayers that could be offered in various circumstances. Trumpets, lutes, harps, tambourines, pipes, and cymbals were among the instruments employed (Ps. 150), and dance was also a part of worship (Ps. 149:3; cf. Judg. 21:21; 2 Sam. 6:14).

There were also individual acts of devotion. Individuals went to the temple to pray, and it can be surmised that they also prayed in their homes. Certainly the presence of a variety of religious objects unearthed by archaeologists in excavated homes suggests this. Prayers were normally offered three times a day in parallel with sacrifices being offered at the temple. Sometimes individuals made special vows and fasted to demonstrate their devotion and as a form of entreaty.

After the destruction of the temple and the end of the sacrificial cult, the synagogue became the gathering place for the community and for individuals to worship. Prayer became the "sacrifice" regularly offered. At the synagogue there seems to have been a ritual that included readings from the Torah, particularly the Ten Commandments and the Shema (Deut. 6:4–9), singing of the psalms, exposition and discussion of sacred texts, and prayer. The service concluded with benedictions offered by the leader.

Synagogue ritual was carried into Christian worship with almost all the same elements appearing. A weekly pattern emerged, complemented by special services to mark special festival days. The pattern of synagogue worship was expanded to include the celebration of the Lord's Supper. Acts of baptism and confirmation became a part of the service at certain times of the year, especially Easter. Daily prayers offered by individuals three times a day followed Jewish patterns and usually included recitation of the Lord's Prayer. Sometimes Christians also assumed the practice of making vows and fasting.

Some Concluding Reflections

When considering worship as presented in the Bible, the acts of devotion cannot, or at least should not, be separated from acts of service, the theme of chapter 12. To worship was to render service to God and to one's neighbor, and, in reverse, such service was understood to be an act of worship.

Nonetheless, there were particular times, places, and activities that structured and constituted the worship of the community and individuals. God was understood to operate within the sphere of time. Thus, a calendar of divine actions to be remembered and celebrated was developed. Festivals of various sorts punctuated that calendar. Times of the month, the week, and the day became important as reminders of God's presence and purpose.

Special places were also important. It was not that God was limited to those places, but rather that those places reminded the people that God had and could meet them within the real world of time and space. Because God's presence had been recognized in certain places, those places became holy, sacred, set apart. Whether the temple, synagogue, church, or home hearth, there were places that people found especially appropriate for worship.

There were numerous expressions of devotion, including sacrifice (eventually to be replaced by prayer), song, dance, reading of and reflection on the traditions passed down through the generations, vows, fasting, and acts of service. Worship was central to life and was rich in its forms of expression.

Questions for Discussion

1. How do you see worship and service as interconnected? Is every form of service also worship? How does service become worship, or vice versa?
2. Why is time so important in the Bible? How does the structuring of time in terms of the liturgical calendar help in worship?
3. How do you experience the reality of sacred space? Are there certain places (in your community or in your house of worship) that seem more holy to you?
4. How many different acts of worship do you recognize and practice in your own community or personal worship? How do these various activities enrich worship?

Chapter Twelve

Service

As was indicated in chapter 11, the themes of service and worship cannot be separated sharply from one another. The terms usually used in Hebrew and Greek for "service" or "worship," for instance, can be translated in English in several different ways. Whether a term should be rendered as "worship" or "service" can often only be decided on the basis of literary context. To perform some types of "service" was to "worship," and one form of "worship" was "service."

Nonetheless, for the sake of presentation, the larger theme of worship/service has been divided in this book into two chapters. Chapter 11 is concentrated more on what might be called liturgical/cultic (i.e., external matters), along with various practices involved in divine worship. Chapter 12 deals more with the manner in which devotion/ethical concern/motivation (i.e., internal matters) issue in worshipful service of God. However, this is, to a large degree, an artificial separation of closely intertwined matters.

The idea of service in the Bible is linked to the understanding that devotion to God is best manifested by specific deeds of adoration at appointed times and places of worship as well as by acts of compassion and assistance to one's neighbors. There is little reflection on service in an abstract manner. The emphasis is on the concrete. When a lawyer/theologian asked Jesus, "Teacher, which commandment in the law is the greatest?" Jesus answered, " 'You shall love the Lord your God will all your heart, and with all your soul, and with all your mind.' This is the greatest and first commandment. And a second is like it: 'You shall love your neighbor as yourself.' On these two commandments hang all the law and the prophets" (Matt. 22:35–40). Jesus' ministry, along with that of numerous other persons in the Bible, demonstrates how these commandments were to be made concrete in the midst of the real world.

The Language of Service

The principal Hebrew term that is translated as "service" or sometimes "worship" is based on the verb *'abad*, which in the first instance means "to work for someone." The noun *'abodah*, derived from the verb, means "work" (freely offered or resulting from enslavement) and "worship." Often it was a slave that rendered the "service" to a master (Exod. 21:2, 6; Jer. 34:14). The verb is used to describe the toil involved in tilling the ground (Gen. 2:5; 4:2–12) or tasks involving an animal (Deut. 15:19). This same verb is used to indicate a variety of ways to honor God in the cult (Exod. 3:12; 23:33; Deut. 6:13; Jer. 5:19).

Sometimes actual slaves are described as doing such "service" (Exod. 12:16; Deut. 23:16; Mal. 1:6), while at other times the "service" is provided by persons subservient to a king, such as servants and advisors, who are not technically indentured in any way (1 Sam. 29:3; 2 Kgs. 22:12). Persons who were not actually "slaves" of another sometimes used this language in polite self-effacement (Gen. 18:3, 5; 33:14; 42:10). The noun *'ebed*, related to the verb *'abad*, could be used to designate an actual slave, or it could refer to a worshiper of God who metaphorically was God's slave.

The corresponding terminology in Greek is in most instances more precise. There are three terms, from different roots, that communicate much of what the terms related to the root *'abad* signify in Hebrew. On the one hand, *latreuo* and *latreia* are used almost exclusively with reference to divine service (i.e., worship) offered to God, one nuance of *'abad* (Luke 2:37; Rom. 1:9; Acts 26:7).

On the other hand, two other terms express various forms of activity of one human to another, sometimes out of commitment to God and at other times simply as a secular act. The first term is the verb *diakoneo* and its noun *diakonia*. These terms were used with reference to the act of service rendered to someone (Matt. 27:55 ["provided for him"]; Acts 19:22 ["helpers"]; Phlm. 13 ["service"]). Sometimes these terms are translated "ministry" (Acts 20:24; 21:19; 2 Cor. 5:18). The name of the biblical office of "deacon" is directly related to the noun *diakonia* (Rom. 12:7).

The second term is the verb *douleuo* and its noun *doulos*. The basic meaning is to perform service as a slave (Matt. 8:9; 10:24; Luke 7:2, 8, 10; 12:37, 43, 45–47). But this term can also be used to speak about service to God, thus displaying some of the ambiguity of the Hebrew *'abad* (Matt. 6:24; Luke 16:13; Rom. 14:18). The actions associated with each of these Greek terms, as with the Hebrew, flow from one's inner convictions, from one's love for God. The concrete response to God's gracious love is to praise God wholeheartedly and to love one's neighbors concretely, compassionately, and generously.

A Defining Metaphor

Underlying much of the language about service in the Bible is a metaphor that is somewhat foreign in the modern world. God is viewed as a great king, and human beings are viewed as slaves or servants of the king. This conception is rooted in the primary form of government shared by most people in antiquity. Whether the smaller city-states prevalent among the Canaanites or the mighty empires of Egypt, Assyria/Babylonia, and Rome, the political model was some variation of a monarchy with a king and his subjects. In Hebrew, the sovereign was called a *melek* (king) and the subject was an *'ebed* (servant/slave). In Greek, the terms were *kurios* (lord) and *doulos* (servant/slave).

This political reality eventually provided a metaphor by which to describe divine-human relationships. Most of the people of the ancient world believed in a multiplicity of deities organized in a hierarchical pantheon. The pantheon was organized with one god in charge, called the "lord/king" (and sometimes "father"), with the other deities subservient, though with a certain degree of autonomy within prescribed limits. In Israel, where the conviction was repeatedly affirmed that there was but one God to revere, such a pantheon was not possible (Deut. 6:4–5).

Nonetheless, one of the primary ways of talking about the God of Israel was as a "king" with a royal court (Ps. 82:1). The prophet envisaged the Lord among the royal court, giving directives affecting the human realm (1 Kgs. 22:19–23). The psalmist wrote, "Declare his [God's] glory among the nations, his marvelous works among all the peoples. For great is the LORD, and greatly to be praised; he is to be revered above all gods" (Ps. 96:3–4). And, "Say among the nations, 'The LORD is king!'" (96:10; cf. 97:1; 98:6; 99:1, 4). Similar language of praise for the king is found in the New Testament (1 Tim. 1:17; 6:15; Rev. 19:16). The subjects of the king are servants or slaves who render service, whether in the divine court or on the earth.

Service in the Bible, then, has a double motivation. On the one hand, service is rendered because one has an obligation to one's sovereign. There is no suggestion in the Bible that Joseph had any love for Pharaoh, but he served the Egyptian sovereign faithfully nonetheless (Gen. 41:37–57). Joseph was Pharaoh's slave. On the other hand, service can be offered freely out of love for the sovereign. The psalmist wrote, "Worship the LORD with gladness; come into his presence with singing. Know that the LORD is God. It is he that made us, and we are his; we are his people, and the sheep of his pasture" (Ps. 100:2–3). Abraham (Ps. 105:6), Moses (Exod. 14:31), David (1 Kgs. 8:66), and many more greater and lesser figures are described as servants/slaves of the Lord God, willingly and joyfully.

In the New Testament, Paul repeatedly described himself as a servant/slave of Jesus Christ (Rom. 1:1; Gal. 1:10; Phil. 1:1). He and others were also servants of God (2 Cor. 6:4; 1 Thess. 3:2; Rev. 1:1). They were obligated because they had been ransomed, but they acted freely by the faith graciously given to them by God (Eph. 2:1–10). Those once "slaves of sin" have by the grace of God "become slaves of righteousness" and thereby freed to new life (Rom. 6:17–18).

In light of this language and imagery, it is indeed remarkable that Jesus would say to his followers:

> This is my commandment, that you love one another as I have loved you. No one has greater love than this, to lay down one's life for one's friends. You are my friends if you do what I command you. I do not call you servants any longer, because the servant does not know what the master is doing; but I have called you friends, because I have made known to you everything that I have heard from my Father. (John 15:12–15)

But it was Christ Jesus who "emptied himself, taking the form of a slave" (Phil. 2:7). In so doing Jesus set the standard for servanthood among his followers and was, according to those who loved him, indeed worthy of faithful service, given out of obligation and out of devotion.

The Servant of the Lord

In the book of Isaiah there are a number of references to a special "servant of the Lord," whose assigned service is instructive in terms of what God's people are expected to do. In the literary context of the exilic Isaiah (chapters 40–55), it is clear that the references are to some portion of the Judean exiles who are being claimed by God for special service. Israel, or some portion of the community, is repeatedly called "my servant" or something similar (e.g., Isa. 41:8–9; 42:1–19; 44:2, 21; 49:3). Often the poetic references are expressed in singular grammatical terminology, though clearly designating Israel, the community, as the servant (e.g., Isa. 41:8–10). This singular language has led some interpreters to consider the "servant" as an individual, and certainly the New Testament related Jesus to this figure (cf. Isa. 53 with Matt. 26:24, 54, 56; Mark 9:12; Luke 18:31; 24:25–27, 46), but the context requires a plural, communal understanding of the figure. Four particular passages (Isa. 42:1–4; 49:1–6; 50:4–9; 52:13–53:12), considered by some scholars as additions to the book, give a good sense of the service/ministry assigned to the servant of the Lord. The first poem places special emphasis on the servant's task of bringing forth justice for the nations (42:1, 3–4). (The KJV translates *mishpat* as "judgment," whereas most more recent translations have "justice.") What might that mean for communal ministry? Earlier in Isaiah readers are urged: "Wash yourselves; make yourselves clean; remove the evil of your doings from before my eyes; cease to do evil, learn to do good; seek justice, rescue the oppressed, defend the orphan, plead for the widow" (Isa. 1:16–17; cf. Amos 2:6–8; 5:10–15; Hos. 4:1–2). Bringing justice to the nations means at least ceasing to commit acts of injustice and dismantling the structures of injustice (Isa. 59:1–15).

The second servant poem (49:1–6) highlights another responsibility given to the servant, namely, to witness to God within "the tribes of Jacob" in order to "restore the survivors of Israel" and to be "a light to the nations, that my [God's] salvation may reach to the end of the earth" (49:6; cf. 48:8). The Lord who is Redeemer, Creator, the Holy One of Israel, is doing a "new thing" that will restore scattered Israel and bring blessing to the nations (43:14–21; 48:6–8, 17). Part of the servant's service, and an ongoing challenge to God's people, is to proclaim God's good news and to live in such a fashion that others will come to belief.

In the third (50:4–9) and fourth (52:13–53:12) poems, the servant is assured of God's care even in the midst of grave suffering. God provided "the tongue of a teacher" and opened the servant's ears to enable the servant to go about the work to be done (50:4). Though there was opposition, the servant remained faithful. God will vindicate the servant (50:7–9). Indeed, the severe suffering of the servant is the very means by which the rulers of the nations are shocked into recognizing the redeeming work of God in their midst (52:14–53:3). The grief and pain of the suffering servant proves to be redemptive (53:4–9). In the end, the servant receives vindication by God "because he [the servant] poured out himself to death, and was numbered with the transgressors; yet he bore the sin of many, and made intercession for the transgressors" (53:12). Such a ministry of identification with the scornful and unworthy for the sake of their redemption, with the grave risk of suffering that it entails, is at the heart of what God's people, God's servant, is called to do.

Justice and reconciliation are of the first order of God's business. God chooses individuals and communities to work, to do service, with the aim of eliminating injustice and bringing forth the light of God's salvation for the nations. Suffering as a result of carrying out this mission demonstrates the commitment of God's servants in their service. Jesus was remembered to have said: "Blessed are you when people revile you and persecute you and utter all kinds of evil against you falsely on my account. Rejoice and be glad, for your reward is great in heaven, for in the same way they persecuted the prophets who were before you" (Matt. 5:11–12).

Particular Acts of Service

There are many specific types of service, and examples of that service, in the Bible. As a way to illustrate the interrelationship of internal convictions with external actions, let us recall the story of Zacchaeus. Zacchaeus was a rich tax collector who had an encounter with Jesus (Luke 19:1–4). Jesus went to eat with Zacchaeus, who was considered a sinner by others in the community (19:7). In response to Jesus, Zacchaeus said, "Look, half of my possessions, Lord, I will give to the poor; and if I have defrauded anyone of anything, I will pay back four times as much." Jesus then said, "Today salvation has come to this house, because he too is a son of Abraham. For the Son of Man came to seek out and to save the lost" (19:8–10). Zacchaeus changed his behavior and reached out to the poor. He sought to redress any injustice he may have worked. Because Jesus became his Lord, Zacchaeus sought to serve in very concrete ways. Isaiah contains a compelling description of what is entailed in God's service. The prophet first criticized the false, hypocritical manner of fasting among the people; their act of worship was rendered useless, even disgusting to the Lord, because their internal attitude was completely wrong (58:1–5). The prophet was not condemning the act of fasting as such, but rather the dissonance between act and motive. Though the people fasted, they continued to act in ways that displeased God. Thus, "Look, you serve your own interest on your fast day, and oppress all your workers. Look, you fast only to quarrel and to fight and to strike with a wicked fist. Such fasting as you do today will not make your voice heard on high" (58:3b-4).

What does God desire? "Is not this the fast that I [God] choose: to loose the bonds of injustice, to undo the thongs of the yoke, to let the oppressed go free, and to break every yoke? Is it not to share your bread with the hungry, and bring the homeless poor into your house; when you see the naked, to cover them, and not to hide yourself from your own kin?" (Isa. 58:6–7; cf. 58:9b-10; Matt. 25:31–46). Micah summed up human responsibility for service with these words: "He [God] has told you, O mortal, what is good; and what does the LORD require of you but to do justice, and to love kindness, and to walk humbly with your God?" (Mic. 6:8).

Isaiah also wrote, "The spirit of the Lord GOD is upon me, because the LORD has anointed me; he has sent me to bring good news to the oppressed, to bind up the brokenhearted, to proclaim liberty to the captives, and release to the prisoners; to proclaim the year of the LORD's favor, and the day of vengeance of our God; to comfort all who mourn" (Isa. 61:1–2). It was this passage, according to Luke, that Jesus read and applied to himself at the outset of his public ministry (Luke 4:16–21). He then continued his service on behalf of God by breaking the oppression of demon possession, disease, and sin (Mark 1:21–34; 2:1–5; 3:1–5; cf. Matt. 7:28–29; 8:16–17; 9:1–8; Luke 4:40–41; 5:17–26), bringing comfort and renewal (Mark 5:35–42; cf. 1 Kgs. 17:17–24; 2 Kgs. 4:18–37; Luke

7:11–17; John 11:1–44), and feeding the hungry (Mark 6:30–44; cf. Matt. 14:13–21; Luke 9:10–17).

At one point in this ministry, Jesus gathered with his disciples and washed their feet, performing the service of a slave (John 13:1–17). Then, according to John, Jesus urged his followers to follow his example in their service to others. What's more, John records a new commandment given by Jesus: "I give you a new commandment, that you love one another. Just as I have loved you, you also should love one another. By this everyone will know that you are my disciples, if you have love for one another" (John 13:34–35; cf. Mark 12:28–34; Matt. 5:43–48; Luke 6:27–36).

In the early church a particular office or position emerged that came to be called "deacon" or "deaconess" (1 Tim. 3:8–13; Phil. 1:1; Rom. 16:1). The duties of these "servers" or "helpers" are not specified, but in one text (Acts 6:1–7) seven persons were selected to oversee the "daily distribution [literally, "daily service"] of food" (6:1, 3). While the term "deacon" is not actually used in Acts, the need for the service described was the type of matter that gave rise to the selection of "deacons." Actually, the "deacons" apparently had more responsibility than simply waiting tables (as might be suggested by the NRSV translation of Acts 6:2), at least if the qualifications spelled out in 1 Timothy are taken into consideration. Despite having specific officers or ministers charged with doing "service," the community as a whole continued to understand service to be their responsibility as well.

Paul referred to his work and that of his associates as "service" (*diakonia*). They were "ministers [servants] of a new covenant" (2 Cor. 3:6). Timothy was called a "good minister [servant] of Christ" (1 Tim. 4:6; cf. Col. 1:7; 4:7; Eph. 6:21). The church was gifted by God with apostles, prophets, evangelists, pastors, and teachers in order "to equip the saints [the community of believers] for the work of ministry [service], for building up the body of Christ" (Eph. 4:11–12; cf. 1 Cor. 12:4–13).

Behavior appropriate to the body of Christ included the "fruit of the Spirit": "love, joy, peace, patience, kindness, generosity, faithfulness, gentleness, and self-control" (Gal. 5:22–23; cf. Phil.

4:8–9). Acts of service flowing from such internal guides were expected: "Let love be genuine; hate what is evil, hold fast to what is good; love one another with mutual affection; outdo one another in showing honor. Do not lag in zeal, be ardent in spirit, serve the Lord. Rejoice in hope, be patient in suffering, persevere in prayer. Contribute to the needs of the saints; extend hospitality to strangers" (Rom. 12:9–13).

This exhortation of Paul to the Romans illustrates again the connection between internal conviction and external service. To render assistance and love to another is to serve the Lord. To resist tyranny and injustice, spiritual or physical, is to serve the Lord. To build up Christ's body, the church, is to serve the Lord. Attitude and action go together. The book of James expresses it this way:

> What good is it, my brothers and sisters, if you say you have faith but do not have works? Can faith save you? If a brother or sister is naked and lacks daily food, and one of you says to them, "Go in peace; keep warm and eat your fill," and yet you do not supply their bodily needs, what is the good of that? So faith by itself, if it has no works, is dead.
>
> But someone will say, "You have faith and I have works." Show me your faith apart from your works, and I by my works will show you my faith. (Jas. 2:14–18).

Some Concluding Reflections

Service and worship are inseparable. Proper worship eventuates in appropriate service. Rightly motivated service is at the same time worship pleasing to God. Only for convenience of presentation in this book have the two concepts been separated.

In the Bible, "service" and "servant" are associated with "sovereign/king" and "master/lord." The form of political governance common in antiquity was used metaphorically to describe the relationship of worshiper/follower with the King of the Universe. Humans are in no way literally slaves of God, but God is sovereign and humans are subservient.

One way to understand what service involves is to consider the assignment of one special "servant of the Lord," who in Isaiah was understood as all or part of Israel, and in the New Testament as Jesus. The tasks of this servant included establishing justice, guiding the nations to God, and suffering on behalf of others. While this service was particularly dramatized by all or part of Israel and then by Jesus, the community as a whole had a continuing responsibility to participate. The full task of service can be summed up in the twofold command to love God fully and to love one's neighbor as oneself.

Questions for Discussion

1. What are some of the ways that service overlaps with worship, and vice versa? How does attitude affect action?
2. What are some of the strengths and weaknesses of using the metaphors of king/servant or master/slave as a way of describing the relationship between God and human beings?
3. How does the figure of the "servant of the Lord" in Isaiah suggest ways that God's people should and can carry forth service in the world?
4. What are some of the concrete services that individuals and communities can carry out in response to God's grace and love?

Chapter Thirteen

Reign of God

The theme "reign of God" is known more widely as the "kingdom of God." To speak of God's dominion or kingship is to talk of God's reign. This idea is expressed frequently in the Bible, particularly in the teachings of Jesus. In one sense, God's reign has to do with God's authority. It is not a "kingdom" or "realm"; it is a matter of relationship, not geography. In this understanding, God's reign is now present and effective.

But the "reign of God," at least in some passages, does seem at times to refer to the "realm" or "region" of God's rule—to a place or a sphere into which one may enter. Further, while sometimes this "reign" is considered already present, in many texts the "reign of God" is clearly something "not yet," something expected to be fully realized only in the future.

In the Synoptic Gospels (Matthew, Mark, and Luke) there are a number of references ascribed to Jesus concerning the reign of God. In Matthew, as was a current practice of piety among Jewish writers of his day, the term "heaven" was usually substituted for the term "God." Thus, Matthew speaks of the "kingdom of heaven." This is not done in Mark or Luke, but there is no essential difference in meaning between "kingdom of God" and "kingdom of heaven" (Matt. 18:4; 19:23; Mark 10:15, 23). Whether Jesus understood the reign of God more in present terms or in future terms is yet debated and will be discussed below.

The biblical understanding of the reign of God affirmed the reality of divine rule in a world that seemed oblivious to such a conviction. But according to the writers of the Bible, if God did indeed reign, then the conduct of both believers and unbelievers was of the utmost importance.

The Old Testament Background

While the actual phrase "the kingdom of the LORD" is used only twice in the First Testament (1 Chron. 28:5; 2 Chron. 13:8), the idea that God is King and has a kingdom and/or reigns is expressed in a number of ways. God is King of all the earth and over all nations (Pss. 47:7–8; 93:1–2; 95:4–5; Isa. 37:16; Jer. 10:7, 10). Further, "the LORD is a great God, and a great King above all gods" (Ps. 95:3; cf. 96:4–5; 97:7). God's reign or kingdom "rules over all" (103:19). All God's works "shall speak of the glory of your [God's] kingdom, and tell of your power, to make known to all people your mighty deeds, and the glorious splendor of your kingdom. Your kingdom is an everlasting kingdom, and your dominion endures throughout all generations" (Ps. 145:11–13). The point is that God has the power and authority to exercise rule over all. God is like a great king. The issue is not so much the "realm" or "territory" of God as it is God's "rule" or "dominion."

As a great king, God is also responsible and able to ensure security and justice (e.g., Pss. 145:14–20; 146:3, 7–9; 147:2–6, 8–11). God is able to require obedience from the rulers of great empires (Isa. 44:28–45:1; Jer. 21:1–10). What's more, God's dominion extends over both the present and the future (Isa. 41:21–29; 43:11–21). In the book of Daniel, King Nebuchadnezzar proclaims, "Truly, your God is God of gods and Lord of kings and a revealer of mysteries, for you [Daniel] have been able to reveal this mystery!" (Dan. 2:47).

Most of the references to God as King in the Old Testament assume or express God's special relationship with Israel. God was the "kingly" protector of Israel (Exod. 15:18; Num. 23:21; Judg. 8:23), and God's reign would continue to bring benefit to Israel in all circumstances (e.g., Obad. 21; Mic. 4:7; Isa. 24:23; 33:22; 41:21). Israel was God's people in a special way, the "apple of his [God's] eye" (Deut. 32:10). This meant that, at times, God's dominion was presented as the means by which Israel was going to gain advantage over other nations (Joel 3:19–21; Hag. 2:20–23; Zech. 14:9–19).

But in other texts the universality of God's reign was declared, with the benefits extending to all peoples. Though not yet actually present, the new era of God's reign would usher in a peaceable kingdom where justice would prevail and all creatures would be able to live in harmony (Isa. 2:2–4; 11:6–9; 65:17–25; Hos. 2:16–23; Ezek. 34:25–28). In some texts, God's future reign will be exercised by a new Davidic king or messiah (Isa. 9:7; 11:1–5; Jer. 30:9; Amos 9:11). God's reign, God's kingdom, is intended for all.

Jesus and the Kingdom of God

There is much debate over what in the First Testament can be claimed to represent the actual teaching of Jesus. Some scholars accept certain teachings as genuine, while other scholars dispute their authenticity. What can be affirmed with reasonable certainty is that the historical Jesus did make some reference to the reign of God and believed that God's reign was made imminent by Jesus' own ministry. Most of the debated texts are found in the Synoptic Gospels, which, while written later than the letters of Paul (probably after 70 CE), nonetheless are the best source available to determine what Jesus probably believed and taught. The scholarly debate will not be reviewed in any detail here, but it is important to understand that whatever has been preserved of Jesus' original teachings has been passed along through the interpretive lenses of the several Gospel writers who addressed the early church.

Mark wrote that the first thing Jesus spoke about after his baptism and temptation in the wilderness was God's reign: "The time is fulfilled, and the kingdom of God has come near; repent, and

believe in the good news" (Mark 1:15; cf. Matt. 3:2; 4:17).
Matthew connected this proclamation with words from Isaiah:
"The people who sat in darkness have seen a great light, and for
those who sat in the region and shadow of death light has dawned"
(Matt. 4:16; cf. Isa. 9:2). And then Matthew added: "Jesus went
throughout Galilee, teaching in their synagogues and proclaiming the good news of the kingdom and curing every disease and
every sickness" (Matt. 4:23; cf. 9:35). Luke, while not using the
term "kingdom of God" at this point in his Gospel, did proclaim
that Jesus began his ministry with other words of Isaiah connected
with the inauguration of a new day:

> "The Spirit of the Lord is upon me, because he has anointed
> me to bring good news to the poor. He has sent me to pro-
> claim release to the captives and recovery of sight to the
> blind, to let the oppressed go free, to proclaim the year of the
> Lord's favor" . . . Then he began to say to them, "Today this
> scripture has been fulfilled in your hearing" (Luke 4:18–19,
> 21; cf. Isa. 61:1–2)

In these texts Jesus seems mainly to have understood the "kingdom" in terms of the reign of God rather than as a realm. Further,
while the reign was at hand or was already operative, it was not
exercised within an earthly kingdom of the sort that might
directly challenge Rome. The Gospel writers do not record any
sayings of Jesus where Jesus called God "King." Given the political climate of his day, to use that language would have been dangerous. According to John, Jesus in fact tried to make clear to
Pilate that any kingship or reign that he might claim was not an
earthly, political realm (John 18:36; cf. 8:23; 19:11; Luke 17:21).
Nonetheless, and probably related to Jesus' sayings about the
reign of God and his relation to it, all the Gospels affirm that Jesus
was crucified under the charge that he was "King of the Jews"
(Mark 15:26; Matt. 27:37; Luke 23:38; John 19:19).
    If not an earthly kingdom, what can be said about this reign of
God, this kingdom of heaven, that Jesus announced? First of all,

each of the Synoptic Gospels saw as one consequence of the proclamation of the good news of God's reign the destruction of the power of evil and the healing of disease (Luke 4:40–44; cf. Matt. 4:23; 9:35; Mark 1:23–26, 40–42). Confronted with the reign of God, demonic powers were overcome and cast out (Matt. 12:22–32; cf. Mark 3:22–32; Luke 11:14–23). Second, the kingdom of God/heaven is especially connected to the "poor in spirit" or simply the "poor" (Matt. 5:3; Luke 4:18; 6:20; 7:22; cf. Jas. 2:5) and "those who are persecuted for righteousness' sake" (Matt. 5:10; Luke 6:22). Righteousness and dedication are defining characteristics of the citizens of the kingdom (Matt. 5:19–20; Luke 9:62). The kingdom belongs to "little children," and those like them, who are humble (Luke 18:16–17; cf. Matt. 18:3–4; 19:13–15; Mark 9:37; 10:13–16). Third, the kingdom is to be sought at all cost above all else (Luke 12:31; cf. Matt. 6:33; Mark 9:47). It is like "treasure hidden in a field" or like a "fine pearl" worth everything that one owns (Matt. 13:44–46). Those who consider their worldly wealth as more important than the kingdom will find it difficult—impossible were it not for God's grace—to enter God's kingdom (Mark 10:17–22; cf. Matt. 19:16–30; Luke 18:18–30).

What one begins to see in the various ways the reign of God is described is a tension that runs in several directions. First, is the kingdom of God a place or is it the sphere of divine rule, dominion, and authority? In most texts the rule of God is indicated by the phrase the "reign of God." But there are a few passages that compromise this understanding somewhat. Spatial imagery was certainly used when, according to Matthew, Jesus said, "For I tell you, unless your righteousness exceeds that of the scribes and Pharisees, you will never enter the kingdom of heaven" (Matt. 5:20). And again, "Not everyone who says to me, 'Lord, Lord,' will enter the kingdom of heaven, but only the one who does the will of my Father in heaven" (7:21; 21:31–32). Or, "I tell you, many will come from east and west and will eat with Abraham and Isaac and Jacob in the kingdom of heaven, while the heirs of the kingdom will be thrown into the outer darkness, where there will be weeping and gnashing of teeth" (8:11). These passages (if Jesus indeed spoke them) suggest that he shared some of the beliefs of his culture that understood God's realm as both a place to be entered and a reign, a dominion, to be accepted.

A second tension is of the same order. Is the reign of God already operative or is it yet to come? Jesus seems to have viewed the kingdom as "near at hand" but still yet to come in its fullness. On the one hand, Luke believed that since the power of God was exerted over demons by Jesus, "the kingdom of God has come to you" (Luke 11:20). And again, in controversy with some Pharisees over when the kingdom was coming, Luke reports that Jesus said, "The kingdom of God is not coming with things that can be observed; nor will they say, 'Look, here it is!' or 'There it is!' For, in fact, the kingdom of God is among you" (Luke 17:20–21). The Gospel of John affirms the understanding of the kingdom as already present by equating entrance into the kingdom with eternal life—a life that begins in the present. John wrote that Jesus, in response to a question about the kingdom posed by Nicodemus, said, "Very truly, I tell you, no one can enter the kingdom of God without being born of water and Spirit" (John 3:5). For John, baptism brought life eternal to the believer (John 5:24; cf. Mark 9:45–47).

But on the other hand, each of the Synoptic Gospels portrays Jesus as still looking for the fullness of God's reign. Jesus enjoined watchfulness on his followers because no one knows the day when God's kingdom will be fully actualized (Matt. 24:36–41; 25:1–13; Mark 13:32–37). Jesus told a parable about the faithful exercise of responsibility while they waited for the kingdom to come because, as the introduction to the parable puts it, "they supposed that the kingdom of God was to appear immediately" (Luke 19:11–27; cf. Matt. 25:14–30). Jesus apparently believed that the fullness of God's reign would come soon (Matt. 9:1; Luke 9:27; 22:16, 30), but it was still not yet. Great turmoil would precede the coming of God's full reign (Matt. 24:29–44; Mark 13:24–32; Luke 21:25–31). In the meantime, Jesus urged his followers to pray to God, "Your kingdom come. Your will be done, on earth as it is in heaven" (Matt. 6:10; cf. Luke 11:2). This suggests that Jesus had a futuristic understanding or expectation regarding the coming of God's reign.

As preserved in the Synoptic Gospels, Jesus' teachings about the reign of God assert several key notions about the new community that Jesus was inaugurating. First, at least in the beginning, Jesus did not understand himself or his community to be challenging the earthly kingdoms of his day. His was not a worldly kingdom (Mark 12:17; John 18:36). Second, the character of God's reign was described in a somewhat counterintuitive fashion. One of Jesus' parables portrayed a king ready to forgive an enormous debt if the debtor in turn forgave a much smaller debt to another (Matt. 18:23–35). This parable recalls the entreaty in the Lord's Prayer to "forgive us our debts, as we also have forgiven our debtors" (Matt. 6:12). In another parable the kingdom of heaven is likened to an employer's unbelievable grace—the choice to pay even the latest arrivals the daily wage—to emphasize God's mercy and care (20:1–16). Finally, Jesus apparently was quite aware that the reality of which he was certain was not obvious to others. Thus, he likened the kingdom of heaven, the reign of God, to a mustard seed and to yeast that did not at first seem to be of much significance (13:31–33).

What's more, Jesus recognized that until the end of the current era, seed scattered could not be certain to bear fruit (Matt. 13:1–9, 18–23; cf. Mark 4:1–9; Luke 8:4–8). But in the end, at the harvest, the wheat will be separated from the weeds (Matt. 13:24–30, 36–43), or to use another metaphor, when the nets are pulled in, the good fish will be kept and the bad fish thrown out (Matt. 13:47–49). But until then, the reality of God's reign can only be known to faith.

Other New Testament Witnesses

In the Pauline letters and a few other writings in the Second Testament there are a few, but not many, remaining passages available for studying the biblical view of the reign of God. Since the Synoptic Gospels were written later than most of the epistles (certainly later than the letters of Paul), it may be that reflection on the kingdom/reign of God in Jesus' teaching was still being digested. The unexpected delay in the coming of God's reign (Matt. 4:17; Luke 9:27) posed problems for the community as it tried to live within the tensions of Christ's teachings.

According to Acts, the earliest proclamation presented two main points: the kingdom of God and the name of Jesus Christ. From the words of the risen Lord (Acts 1:3) to the preaching of Philip, Barnabas, and Paul (Acts 8:12; 14:22; 19:8; 20:25; 28:23, 31), Christ's name and the reign of God were presented together as the good news. From the way the term appears in these passages the basic Old Testament understanding of God's reign is presumed. The present reality of the risen Lord was proclaimed, and with it came a clear future expectation that included the consummation of God's purpose with the return of Christ.

In the life of the early church the preaching about the reign of God, while eagerly accepted, raised some significant issues. In some of his earliest letters, 1 and 2 Thessalonians, for instance, Paul found it necessary to address pastoral words to some of his followers concerning this very matter. Some people had loved ones who had died. They feared that their loved ones would not be able to participate in the fullness of God's reign since their death preceded the expected return of Christ. On the one hand, Paul assured them that the day of the Lord had not yet come, contrary to what some people were saying, but on the other hand, when it did arrive, after many difficulties, all—believers who had died and believers yet alive—would be gathered to the Lord (1 Thess. 4:13–18; 2 Thess. 2:1–8). That was Paul's confidence and should be theirs as well. After all, they were to remember that it was God who called them "into his own kingdom and glory" (1 Thess. 2:12). Any "persecutions and afflictions" that the community faced were intended to make them "worthy" of the kingdom of God (2 Thess. 1:4–5; cf. 2 Tim. 4:1, 18; cf. Acts 14:22).

The whole matter of worthiness raised another issue. In Corinth the church was embroiled in a controversy over several matters. Some people were challenging Paul's authority. Paul responded by reminding the Corinthians that "the kingdom of God depends not on talk but on power" and that he was their "father" (1 Cor. 4:15, 20). Further, Paul reprimanded his flock for filing lawsuits against one another, for wronging and defrauding one another (6:1–8). And then he wrote, "Do you not know that wrongdoers will not inherit the kingdom of God? Do not be deceived! Fornicators, idolaters, adulterers, male prostitutes, sodomites, thieves, the greedy, drunkards, revilers, robbers— none of these will inherit the kingdom of God" (6:9–10; cf. Gal. 5:21; Eph. 5:5). Had Paul stopped his argument at this point he would have left the issue as totally a moralistic, legalistic matter. Thankfully, however, he continued: "And this is what some of you used to be. But you were washed, you were sanctified, you were justified in the name of the Lord Jesus Christ and in the Spirit of our God" (1 Cor. 6:11; cf. Rom. 5:1–11; Col. 1:13).

Later when the Christians in Rome became embroiled over the matter of whether certain days were to be set aside as special or certain foods set aside as impure, Paul chided his readers for judging one another's behavior (Rom. 14:1–12). Nothing in itself is clean or unclean (14:14), but

> if your brother or sister is being injured by what you eat, you are no longer walking in love. Do not let what you eat cause the ruin of one for whom Christ died. So do not let your good be spoken of as evil. For the kingdom of God is not food and drink but righteousness and peace and joy in the Holy Spirit. The one who thus serves Christ is acceptable to God and has human approval. Let us then pursue what makes for peace and for mutual upbuilding. (14:15–19)

Among other things, these controversies show that the issue had clearly emerged concerning the kinds of behavior that should be pursued by those seeking inclusion in the reign of God.

There was another issue debated by the Corinthians that Paul felt compelled to address. Some apparently were questioning the fact of Christ's resurrection (1 Cor. 15:12). Paul responded vigorously that Christ has been raised from the dead and would, at his return, raise all those who belong to him (15:23). Then "comes the end, when he [Christ] hands over the kingdom to God the Father, after he has destroyed every ruler and every authority and power. For he must reign until he has put all his enemies under his feet. The last enemy to be destroyed is death" (15:24–26). God alone can raise the dead to imperishable life because otherwise "flesh and blood cannot inherit the kingdom of God" (15:50).

In the last book of the Bible, the book of Revelation, two dramatic affirmations are made. First, the struggling, small, insignificant community of Jesus' followers scattered around the Mediterranean Sea was declared through Christ "to be a kingdom, priests serving his [Christ's] God and Father" (Rev. 1:6; cf. 5:10; 1 Pet. 2:9–10). To be called priests may not sound so startling, but to be identified as God's kingdom, as the dominion of God, as the reign of God, particularly over against the Roman Empire, was astounding. Second, as the apocalyptic vision of divine judgment against the evil powers of the world unfolded, after the seventh angel blew his trumpet, loud heavenly voices cried out, "The kingdom of the world has become the kingdom of our Lord and of his Messiah, and he will reign forever and ever" (11:15). Despite all the power of Rome, God's will would prevail and justice would come, "destroying those who destroy the earth" (11:18).

Some Concluding Reflections

The First Testament presents the reign of God as one metaphor for God's relationship with the world. As a king of a worldly kingdom, God protected and guided his people and exercised just reign over them. In the course of time, God's reign took on a more universal tone with a future orientation. To depict God as King was one way to describe God's relationship with humanity, but not a great deal more was made of God's reign.

In the Second Testament most of the references to the kingdom of God are in words ascribed to Jesus. Jesus affirmed the importance of God's reign for the present and the future. The reign of God brought healing, forgiveness, justice, and peace. The kingdom was in the midst of human community, but it was also still on the horizon. Lives were changed and communities were challenged. According to Jesus, the reign of God was not something political or worldly, but nonetheless it could be sought, and it required sacrifice.

In the remainder of the New Testament only a limited number of references are made to the reign of God. The same tensions are found between the reign of God being something yet in the future and being a power affecting the present. Behavior is changed when there is an expectation of a glorious and just reign that will one day be extended over the whole world.

Questions for Discussion

1. What difference does it make if the term "reign of God" means a "kingdom" in terms of place or in terms of the character of the governance experienced?
2. How can the tension between Jesus' teachings about the present reality of God's reign be reconciled with his words about the kingdom that was yet to come?
3. What are some of the things that Jesus said about the kingdom that surprise you? Why?
4. What kinds of behavior are expected of those who participate in God's kingdom? How can the reign of God be extended to others and confirmed by the way God's people live?